Aquarium

33 1/3 Global

33 1/3 Global, a series related to but independent from **33 1/3**, takes the format of the original series of short, music-based books and brings the focus to music throughout the world. With initial volumes focusing on Japanese and Brazilian music, the series will also include volumes on the popular music of Australia/Oceania, Europe, Africa, the Middle East, and more.

33 1/3 Japan

Series Editor: Noriko Manabe

Spanning a range of artists and genres—from the 1970s rock of Happy End to technopop band Yellow Magic Orchestra, the Shibuya-kei of Cornelius, classic anime series *Cowboy Bebop,* J-Pop/EDM hybrid Perfume, and vocaloid star Hatsune Miku—**33 1/3 Japan** is a series devoted to in-depth examination of Japanese popular music of the twentieth and twenty-first centuries.

Published Titles:

Supercell's *Supercell* by Keisuke Yamada

AKB48 by Patrick W. Galbraith and Jason G. Karlin

Yoko Kanno's *Cowboy Bebop Soundtrack* by Rose Bridges

Perfume's *Game* by Patrick St. Michel

Cornelius's *Fantasma* by Martin Roberts

Joe Hisaishi's *My Neighbor Totoro: Soundtrack* by Kunio Hara

Shonen Knife's *Happy Hour* by Brooke McCorkle

Nenes' *Koza Dabasa* by Henry Johnson

Yuming's *The 14th Moon* by Lasse Lehtonen

Forthcoming Titles:

Yellow Magic Orchestra's *Yellow Magic Orchestra* by Toshiyuki Ohwada

Kohaku utagassen: The Red and White Song Contest by Shelley Brunt

Toshiko Akiyoshi-Lew Tabackin Big Band's *Kogun* by E. Taylor Atkins

S.O.B.'s *Don't Be Swindle* by Mahon Murphy and Ran Zwigenberg

33 1/3 Brazil

Series Editor: Jason StanyekCovering the genres of samba, tropicália, rock, hip hop, forró, bossa nova, heavy metal and funk, among others, **33 1/3 Brazil** is a series devoted to in-depth examination of the most important Brazilian albums of the twentieth and twenty-first centuries.

Published Titles:

Caetano Veloso's *A Foreign Sound* by Barbara Browning

Tim Maia's *Tim Maia Racional Vols. 1 &2* by Allen Thayer

João Gilberto and Stan Getz's *Getz/Gilberto* by Brian McCann

Gilberto Gil's *Refazenda* by Marc A. Hertzman

Dona Ivone Lara's *Sorriso Negro* by Mila Burns

Milton Nascimento and Lô Borges's *The Corner Club* by Jonathon Grasse

Racionais MCs' *Sobrevivendo no Inferno* by Derek Pardue

Naná Vasconcelos's *Saudades* by Daniel B. Sharp

Chico Buarque's First *Chico Buarque* by Charles A. Perrone

Forthcoming titles:

Jorge Ben Jor's *África Brasil* by Frederick J. Moehn

33 1/3 Europe

Series Editor: Fabian Holt

Spanning a range of artists and genres, **33 1/3 Europe** offers engaging accounts of popular and culturally significant albums of Continental Europe and the North Atlantic from the twentieth and twenty-first centuries.

Published Titles:

Darkthrone's *A Blaze in the Northern Sky* by Ross Hagen

Ivo Papazov's *Balkanology* by Carol Silverman

Heiner Müller and Heiner Goebbels's *Wolokolamsker Chaussee* by Philip V. Bohlman

Modeselektor's *Happy Birthday!* by Sean Nye

Mercyful Fate's *Don't Break the Oath* by Henrik Marstal

Bea Playa's *I'll Be Your Plaything* by Anna Szemere and András Rónai

Various Artists' *DJs do Guetto* by Richard Elliott

Czesław Niemen's *Niemen Enigmatic* by Ewa Mazierska and Mariusz Gradowski

Massada's *Astaganaga* by Lutgard Mutsaers

Los Rodriguez's *Sin Documentos* by Fernán del Val and Héctor Fouce

Édith Piaf's *Récital 1961* by David Looseley

Nuovo Canzoniere Italiano's *Bella Ciao* by Jacopo Tomatis

Iannis Xenakis's *Persepolis* by Aram Yardumian

Vopli Vidopliassova's *Tantsi* by Maria Sonevytsky

Amália Rodrigues's *Amália at the Olympia* by Lila Ellen Gray

Ardit Gjebrea's *Projekt Jon* by Nicholas Tochka

Aqua's *Aquarium* by C.C. McKee

Forthcoming Titles:

J.M.K.E.'s *To the Cold Land* by Brigitta Davidjants

Taco Hemingway's *Jarmark* by Kamila Rymajdo

Tripes' *Kefali Gemato Hrisafi* by Dafni Tragaki

Silly's *Februar* by Michael Rauhut

CCCP's *Fedeli Alla Linea's 1964-1985 Affinità-Divergenze Fra Il Compagno Togliatti E Noi Del Conseguimento Della Maggiore Età* by Giacomo Bottà

33 1/3 Oceania

Series Editors: Jon Stratton (senior editor) and Jon Dale (specializing in books on albums from Aotearoa/New Zealand)Spanning a range of artists and genres from Australian Indigenous artists to Maori and Pasifika artists, from Aotearoa/New Zealand noise music to Australian rock, and including music from Papua and other Pacific islands, **33 1/3 Oceania** offers exciting accounts of albums that illustrate the wide range of music made in the Oceania region.

Aquarium

C.C. McKee

Series Editor: Fabian Holt

BLOOMSBURY ACADEMIC
NEW YORK • LONDON • OXFORD • NEW DELHI • SYDNEY

BLOOMSBURY ACADEMIC
Bloomsbury Publishing Inc
1385 Broadway, New York, NY 10018, USA
50 Bedford Square, London, WC1B 3DP, UK
29 Earlsfort Terrace, Dublin 2, Ireland

BLOOMSBURY, BLOOMSBURY ACADEMIC and the Diana logo are
trademarks of Bloomsbury Publishing Plc

First published in the United States of America 2024

Bloomsbury Publishing Inc does not have any control over, or
responsibility for, any third-party websites referred to or in this book. All
internet addresses given in this book were correct at the time of going
to press. The author and publisher regret any inconvenience caused if
addresses have changed or sites have ceased to exist, but can accept no
responsibility for any such changes.

Whilst every effort has been made to locate copyright holders the
publishers would be grateful to hear from any person(s) not here
acknowledged.

A catalog record for this book is available from the Library of Congress.

ISBN: HB: 978-1-5013-8417-2
PB: 978-1-5013-8418-9
ePDF: 978-1-5013-8420-2
eBook: 978-1-5013-8419-6

Typeset by Deanta Global Publishing Services, Chennai, India
Printed and bound in Great Britain

Series: 33 1/3 Europe

To find out more about our authors and books visit www.bloomsbury.com
and sign up for our newsletters.

Contents

Acknowledgments

This book began in 2020 during Covid lockdown when the effusive cheeriness of Bubblegum Eurodance provided some frivolity amidst unfathomable loss and uncertainty. Diving into the world of Aqua was not merely a nostalgia trip back to late 1990s adolescence but also a means of exploring my enduring hunch that there was something queer about *Aquarium* that I could never quite put my finger on. As I (over)shared my discoveries and recollections with friends and colleagues, I learned that I was by no means alone in feeling something resonant (but unsettled) in Aqua's camp. Over the course of writing, researching, and collaborating, I also came to embrace a facet of myself that was hard to pinpoint. In some ways, the queer and trans camp I engage in this project reflects the beginning of my own transition and the community that has made it possible.

My immense gratitude goes out to Christian Møller, A&R director at Universal Music Denmark, whose response to my request for interviews with the band sparked a series of conversations that were instrumental to the book's narrative. My thanks to those who were "behind the scenes" of *Aquarium*, but no less integral to Aqua's success, for their willingness to speak candidly and offer their stories: Niclas Anker, Karsten Delgado, Tatsuya Nakamoto, Jens-Otto Paludan, and Peter Stenbæk. I also had the distinguished pleasure of interviewing the band over the course of Fall 2022; thank you to René Dif, Lene Nystrøm, and Søren Rasted for engaging and contributing to this project.[1] My thanks also go to the reviewer and colleagues who commented on the manuscript, and Emily Shoyer who acted as a research assistant. This book would have suffered without their insights.

My sincere thanks to Falk Springer, a dear friend and creative collaborator, and Hendrik Wolff, of Warning in Berlin, for facilitating the realization of an Aqua cover project that bolsters the queer dimension of this book as a creative archive. I also extend deep gratitude to the artists who contributed to the cover record: Murat Önen, Ariel Zetina, and Paula Nacif, Callum Magnum, Evelyn and Scotia, The Moon Baby and J-Cow, and peachlyfe, KimKim, and Proxy Server. It has been a pleasure to work together to explore Aqua's queer afterlives with an ear to the dancefloor.

This book is dedicated to those queer ravers in Philadelphia and beyond with a flair for the DIY and impeccably bad taste. They enthusiastically supported this project from its inception with critical conversations about 1990s Eurodance at all hours of the night.

[1] Claus Norreen, who has not been involved with Aqua since 2016, politely declined my request for an interview.

Introduction
I'm a *Camp* Girl

The twenty-fifth anniversary of Aqua's debut album *Aquarium* marked a resurgence of the band in popular consciousness. In 2022, the video for "Barbie Girl" surpassed one billion views on YouTube. Aqua expanded their touring schedule across Europe, North, and South America. Most recently, "Barbie Girl" was sampled on the Nicki Minaj and Ice Spice track, "Barbie World," for the soundtrack to Greta Gerwig's 2023 *Barbie* movie. Aqua's stand-out song has cemented itself, whether popular taste would admit, as a quintessential late 1990s hit in a moment when electronic music made its way out of the club and rave, superseding rock at the top of the pop charts. The track's infectious beat and unforgettable chorus were ubiquitous on airwaves across the world and distilled the optimism of the economic boom that followed the end of the Cold War and rise of multicultural globalism in the 1990s. The song heralded Aqua's expansion beyond Scandinavia and was released as a single shortly after *Aquarium* hit the shelves in Europe on March 26, 1997. The Danish-Norwegian band—comprised of vocalist Lene Nystrøm, rapper René Dif, and composer-musicians Claus Norreen and Søren Rasted—formed in Copenhagen two years before, in 1995 (Figure 1). The rise of rave music was an integral part of their foundation, and Aqua gained early notoriety as dynamic club performers throughout Denmark.

Figure 1 *Aqua in the studio, photograph from 1996 to 1997, reproduced from the collection of Karsten Delgado.*

As the album circulated, so too did its flagship single, skyrocketing to the top of the Danish charts and remaining in the top 40 for a year and a half. Within 2 weeks, the album went double-platinum in Denmark with sales of more than 100,000 copies, putting it in 1 in 12 homes. Both *Aquarium* and "Barbie Girl" peaked at the top of the charts first throughout Europe, then Asia with the release of the single in May 1997, and subsequently in the United Kingdom, the United States, Canada, Australia, and New Zealand in the late summer and early fall.[1] In the span of nine months, Aqua went from weekend tours of Denmark's discotheques to global fame,

[1] "European Top 100 Albums," and "Top National Sellers," *Music and Media* 14 & 15 (1997, 1998); "Billboard Hot 100," "Billboard 200," "Radio Songs," "Billboard Canadian Albums," *Billboard* (1997–8); "Top 100 Singles," "Top 100 Albums," *ARIA* (1997–8).

multi-platinum records, and one of the most (in)famous dance singles of the late twentieth century.

This book traces the history of *Aquarium* from Aqua's formation, their discovery by Universal Denmark, and their meteoric ascent over the course of 1997 and 1998. To tell this story, I situate Aqua's debut within a set of concentric musical contexts. First, Aqua's ability to captivate audiences across the world necessitates comparisons with other international anglophone pop stars of the period—Spice Girls, Backstreet Boys, Britney Spears, and the like. Second, Aqua's distinctive ability to blend pop music structures with the thumping beats of dance is indebted to the Eurodance that had developed over the decade with its characteristic house-derived basslines and anthemic vocals. Thus, I temper Aqua's reputation as a sugary sweet pop band geared toward adolescent listeners by returning *Aquarium* to the context of crossover tracks that worked on the dancefloor as well as the playground. Finally, I narrow this continental scope further to acknowledge the unique Bubblegum dance scene that coalesced in mid-1990s Denmark, comparing *Aquarium* to other acts from the period demystifies Aqua's singularity by situating them in a field of contemporaries.[2]

Analyses of the album's singles structure this historical narrative to argue that the significance of *Aquarium* for pop musical history emerges from a *camp sensibility* that permeates not only the album itself but also a set of listening practices that push it into the realm of the queer. Even before the renewed

_____

[2] Kim Cooper and David Smay, eds., *Bubblegum Music, is the Naked Truth* (Los Angeles: Feral House, 2001), 224, 261, 265, 294.

interest in *Aquarium*, queer listeners held onto the album in the form of DJ mixes, at house parties, and guilty pleasures replayed in private. In what follows, I offer a summary overview of camp, and its relationship to queer culture and theory, that will be expanded and nuanced over the course of this book.

Camp is a covert reading practice that developed within modern queer subcultures, using irony, parody, and pastiche to extract and create coded, internal meanings about sexuality, gender, and culture from popular media that had little or nothing to do with queerness, at least on face value. By most accounts, camp emerged in the gay communities of late nineteenth-century England; its use as an adjective dates back at least to 1909, where it was defined as "addicted to 'actions and gestures of exaggerated emphasis; pleasantly ostentatious or, in manner, affected.'" By 1945 camp, as it was used in the United States, connoted a particular form of homosexuality.[3] Novelist Christopher Isherwood brought further nuance to the concept by distinguishing two distinct modes: low camp was "un utterly debased form" associated with the theatrical and the nelly, "a swishy little boy with peroxided hair, dressed in a picture hat and feather boa, pretending to be Marlene Dietrich"; high camp, which could be either gay or straight, expressed "what's basically serious to you in terms of fun and artifice and elegance."[4] Therefore, when Susan Sontag published her "Notes on 'Camp'" in 1964, the aesthetic sensibility and its canon were freighted

[3]William White, "'Camp' as Adjective: 1909–1966," *American Speech* 41 (1966): 70–2.
[4]Christopher Isherwood, *The World in the Evening* (New York: Noonday Press, 1954), 110.

with at least half a century of use in homosexual discourse where it became a means of moving through the world by coopting objects from a heterosexual cultural landscape. Sontag drew a loose perimeter around camp as "something of a private code, a badge of identity even, among small urban cliques" rooted in failed seriousness, a love of artifice and exaggeration that privileges surface style over content, and a form of reading that is fundamentally "disengaged, depoliticized—or at least apolitical."[5] Sontag acknowledges the relationship between homosexuality and camp in the "Notes," but minimizes the extent to which it emerged from gay and lesbian communities.

Sontag's elucidation opened a slew of popular intellectual engagements from the straight world in the 1960s and 1970s, where camp's exclusive legibility, limited to an elite few in the know, was particularly alluring. The intelligentsia could, therefore, engage popular culture from a remove because camp, as Sontag famously characterized it, "sees everything in quotation marks."[6] The heterosexualization of camp accompanied the gay community's movement away from it after the 1969 Stonewall riots on the basis that camp only obliquely recognized homosexuality through oppressive representations and was insufficient to moving the gay liberation movement's political goals "out of the closet." In the era of disco, the mustachioed gay clone, and radical lesbian

---

[5] Susan Sontag, "Notes on 'Camp,'" in *Against Interpretation and Other Essays* (New York: Farrar, Straus, and Giroux, 1966), 275, 277.
[6] Ibid., 280.

feminism, camp was frequently deemed a vestige of the fairy's open secret.[7]

Camp returned to gay, lesbian, and queer discourse in the late 1980s and early 1990s with the rise of the HIV/AIDS epidemic. Sontag's "Notes" became a strawman because of its popularity as a seminal text for the proliferation of pop or het camp in the 1970s. Gay, feminist, and queer theorists reclaimed a camp that was inherently (rather than circumstantially) queer by shadowboxing Sontag's definition of camp as apolitical and bourgeois. With the medicalized stigmatization of queer subcultures in the 1980s, a re-politicized camp became a means of lodging an oppositional critique through parody. Theorists like Richard Dyer articulated a politics of camp in the past, "a kind of going public or coming out before the emergence of gay liberationist politics."[8] Andrew Ross saw camp as a means for gay intellectuals to press against "this dialectic between personal liberation and corporate-State regulation (of medical technologies, etc.)" in the era of HIV.[9]

The emergence of queer theory from activist circles in the 1980s and early 1990s brought complications to the limitation of camp as a gay cis-male practice largely predicated on exaggerated (cis-)femininity. Judith Butler's 1990 *Gender Trouble* offered a pathbreaking interpretation of gender as a performed social construct preceding and structuring the

---

[7] Andrew Britton, "For Interpretation, Against Camp," in *Camp: Queer Aesthetics and the Performing Subject: A Reader*, ed. Fabio Cleto (Edinburgh: University of Edinburgh Press, 1999), 136–42.

[8] Richard Dyer, *Heavenly Bodies: Film Stars and Society* (New York: St. Martin's Press, 1986), 115.

[9] Andrew Ross, *No Respect: Intellectuals and Popular Culture* (New York: Taylor and Francis, 1989), 144.

assumed biological "fact" of sex. "In other words," Butler says, "acts, gestures, and desires produce the effect of an internal core or substance, but produce this *on the surface* of the body." Although camp itself remains in the background of Butler's theory, the camp art form of drag is central because it "effectively mocks both the expressive model of gender and the notion of a true gender identity." Gender, then is "a corporeal style" performed by the body as a "*stylized repetition of acts* (emphasis in the original)."[10]

The parodic status of gender as a political performance on the surface of the body opened the possibility for camp to take on new political possibilities in feminist and queer cultural critique.[11] Moreover, there are camp resonances in queer of color critiques that engage gender parody even when the concept is not explicitly evoked. For instance, José Esteban Muñoz's theorization of disidentification offers alternative ways into queer performativities from the subversive reconfiguration of cultural objects' capacity to signify akin, but not identical, to camp. Muñoz defines disidentification as "the hermeneutical performance of decoding mass, high, or any other cultural field from the perspective of a minority subject who is disempowered in such a representational hierarchy."[12] Although camp itself again took a backseat in queer theory after the turn of the millennium, these scholars

[10] Judith Butler, *Gender Trouble: Feminism and the Subversion of Identity* (New York: Routledge, 1990), 185, 186, 190–1.

[11] Cleto, *Camp*; Moe Meyer, ed., *The Poetics and Politics of Camp* (New York: Routledge, 1994); Pamela Robertson, *Guilty Pleasures: Feminist Camp from Mae West to Madonna* (Durham: Duke University Press, 1996).

[12] José Esteban Muñoz, *Disidentifications: Queers of Color and the Performance of Politics* (Minneapolis: University of Minnesota Press, 1999), 25.

laid the foundation for others to integrate the specificity of a transgender perspective into camp discourses and the objects that fall under its purview. Most recently, queer scholars Marissa Brostoff and Sid Cunningham have sought to redress the two-dimensional, tragedy-driven treatment of transgender lives by embracing these failures to convey the fullness of transness with camp's politics of humor.[13] As Cunningham puts it, "I would argue that camp can serve similarly to enjoy the space mainstream representation allows for transness while organizing dissensus with the underwhelming ends to which our stories and images are mobilized."[14]

The elucidation of a trans camp that has always dwelt within a queer approach nuances the concept to account for the parodies of gender that do not only rest on the surface of the body, but also live within it.

This book is in conversation with other contemporary histories of camp that hold multiple and contradictory conceptualizations in tension, while also allowing for the personal to inflect the analysis.[15] Camp allows us to take *Aquarium* on its own terms while also attending to its reception by minoritarian listeners often obscured in pop cultural discourses. My argument for the utility of queering and

[13] Marissa Brostoff, "Notes on Caitlyn, or Genre Trouble: On the Continued Usefulness of Camp as Queer Method," *Differences: A Journal of Feminist Cultural Studies* 28, no. 3 (2017): 1–18.

[14] Sid Cunningham, "'Something to Disclose'—Notes on *Disclosure and the Possibility of Trans Camp*," *Jump Cut: A Review of Contemporary Media* no. 60 (Spring 2021), https://www.ejumpcut.org/archive/jc60.2021/Cunningham -Disclosure/index.html.

[15] Paul Baker, *Camp!: The Story of the Attitude that Conquered the World* (London: Footnote Press, 2023).

camping Aqua could easily slide into a singular mode of "auto-analysis"—that is, this white, millennial, trans-femme author hears queer camp as a result of their relation to the album. However, as Freya Jarman-Ivens reminds us, auto-analysis is a productive ground from which arise "possibilities regarding the relationship between sonic events and theoretical processes," where personal subcultural practices furnish critical "examples of how identification with voices might work in real listening."[16] Additionally, one apocryphal anecdote that promised to substantiate a historical continuity in Aqua's queer appeal swirled around the early research for this book: "Barbie Girl" was introduced to the United States through gay clubs during the spring of 1997. Interviews with key members of Aqua's team at MCA confirm the veracity of this calculated move—where extended and remixed versions of the track were pressed on promo white-label vinyl—orchestrated in conjunction with American Universal marketing employees Eamon Sherlock and Carmen Cattatori.[17] Therefore, American interest in Aqua was cultivated within the queer community, a demographic with a flexible income, a long history as club-going dance music tastemakers, and an affinity for camp that will emerge as a central point of convergence between commercial success and mixed critical reception.

Despite this "smoking gun" that ties *Aquarium* to a specifically queer subset of listeners in the late 1990s, the queer voices

---

[16] Freya Jarman-Ivens, *Queer Voices: Technologies, Vocalities, and the Musical Flaw* (New York: Palgrave MacMillan, 2011).

[17] Jens-Otto Paludan, Interview with the author, February 18, 2022; Niclas Anker, Interview with the author, August 21, 2022.

themselves were overwhelmingly absent from the archive.[18] Over the course of researching and writing this book, a host of queer listeners emerged from the woodwork to proclaim their affinity for the album. In order to analytically substantiate the latent queerness that I argue percolates without full expression in Aqua's debut, this book was written in tandem with my curation of a creative archive comprised of five covers executed by contemporary queer electronic musicians from Europe and North America.[19] Analyses of each cover in relation to Aqua's original song and the remixes released with each single will serve as both litmus test for and expansion of my own interpretation. As derivative musical acts, the cover and remix retain much of the structure and form of the "original." The cover uniquely adapts the covering artist's style and subtly inflects the song with new meaning by reperforming the instrumentation and vocals. The remix, by contrast, loosens the constraints of presumptive originality with the song's original elements (or stems); it proliferates authorship such that the track emerges as a network of simulacra; its reduction of vocals to riffs accentuates the tendency to explore a track's abstract elements.[20] I propose this musical intervention as a creative and collective gesture that expands upon other investigations of queer pop listenership, Sasha Geffen's most

[18] In recent years, Aqua has explicitly leaned into their queer fandom, recording and performing a cover of "I Am What I Am"—a camp classic written for the Broadway musical *La Cage aux Folles* and popularized by disco diva Gloria Gaynor—for the 2021 World Pride celebration in Copenhagen.

[19] The cover album will be released digitally and on vinyl through Warning record label in Berlin.

[20] Eduardo Navas, *Remix Theory: The Aesthetics of Sampling* (New York: Springer, 2012), 37–42.

notable among them, and reaches back into our memories of Aqua to foreground the queerness we found there despite being sublimated in the original discourse surrounding the album.[21]

The book proceeds chronologically, each chapter centering on one single from *Aquarium*. They offer entwined analyses of the song and its accompanying video as two facets of a whole production where camp is self-consciously produced by the band themselves as well as the queer listener who intervenes with supplementary interpretations. In addition to employing queerness to read Aqua's *Aquarium*, this book also extends camp outside of its usual visual focus and into the musical. Academic studies devoted to music and camp have been instrumental in incorporating queer theory into pop musicology by rethinking the relationship between text (or score) and context, focusing on *how* a song is performed in addition to *what* the performance is.[22] Reading *Aquarium* as a confluence of musical and visual allows us to trace the imbricated forms of camp that coexist in Aqua's production. I augment this historical narrative with an analytic strand that

[21] Sasha Geffen, *Glitter Up the Dark: How Pop Music Broke the Binary* (Austin: University of Texas Press, 2020).

[22] Stan Hawkins, "Dragging Out Camp: Narrative Agendas in Madonna's Musical Production," in *Madonna's Drowned Worlds: New Approaches to her Cultural Transformations, 1983–2003*, ed. Freya Jarman-Ivans and Santiago Fouz-Hernandez (Burlington: Ashgate, 2004), 3–21; Katrin Horn, *Women, Camp, and Popular Culture: Serious Excess* (London: Palgrave MacMillan, 2017); Freya Jarman-Ivens, "Notes on Musical Camp," in *The Ashgate Research Companion to Popular Music*, ed. Derek B. Scott (Burlington, VT: Ashgate Publishing, 2009), 189–203. Christopher Moore and Philip Purvis, eds., *Music & Camp* (Middletown, CT: Wesleyan University Press, 2018); Jodi Taylor, *Playing it Queer: Popular Music, Identity, and Queer World-Making* (New York: Peter Lang, 2012).

moves along two parallel streams of interpretation. On the one hand, I read a pop camp sensibility in *Aquarium* that failed to realize its queer potential. On the other, this failure doubles back on itself to eke out possibilities for the nimble contours of queer camp to emerge in the multivalence of parody. Presented together, these approaches trace Aqua's success and take *Aquarium* seriously—or as seriously as one can—as a pathbreaking album entwined with millennial queerness that touches the camp of Bubblegum dance.

1 I'm a *Bubblegum* Girl

When Aqua rocketed to global stardom in 1997, they joined a group of Danish dance-pop acts with an explicitly international focus rooted in infectious melodies and straightforward English-language lyrics about love, loss, and the ennui of everyday life. Denmark's Swedish neighbors are better known for their export of Scandi-pop acts from Abba and Ace of Base to Max Martin's production of groups like Britney Spears and the Backstreet Boys at the renowned Cheiron Studios. Nevertheless, a Danish strain of international pop music emerged in the wake of the international proliferation of hip-hop and the 1988–9 Second Summer of Love in the UK that presaged rock's supersession by electronic music.

In 1990, the dance and hip-hop group Cut'n'Move achieved international success with their debut single "Get Serious," a mid-tempo disco-inflected house track that alternates between rapped and soulfully sung verses with an infectious piano chord hook taken from the 1978 Soul Train classic "Dance to the Drummer's Beat" and an organ riff from "Land of 1000 Dances," popularized by 1960s R&B singer Wilson Pickett. Although their sound was distinct from Aqua's, Cut'n'Move's deft translation of Black American disco, R&B, and rap into contemporary dance hits paved an important path for *Aquarium's* strategic musical collage.

The most direct stylistic predecessors to Aqua hit the scene in the years just preceding the release of *Aquarium*. In 1994, Whigfield (Danish singer Sannie Carlson and Italian producer Larry Pignagnoli) released the weekender anthem "Saturday Night" globally, though it had been out in Italy since 1992. The following year the sister duo Me & My (Susanne and Pernille Georgi) released their shiny and upbeat "Dub-i-dub" which took them to the top of the global charts. Both tracks feature the prominent use of atypical synth patches and non-lexical hooks—for Whigfield "Dee dee na na na?" and "Dub-i-dub-i-dub-i-dub-dub-dub" for Me & My—that would come to characterize the subgenre.

Where Cut'n'Move and Whigfield drew attention to the Danish music scene abroad, Kenneth Bager was an influential DJ and musician who brought British acid house and early techno to Denmark. "Kaos," the 1989 hit by his group Dr. Baker, layers Spanish spoken word about drugs and terrorism with verses rapped by the Afro-Danish DJ Natasja Saad, an acid synth line, and pounding bass. The subsequent "Turn Up the Music" (1991) is a lighthearted sax and piano house track blended with verses rapped by the Ugandan-Danish Al Agami. Bager then translated these elements into the distinctive Danish Bubblegum dance sound as the founder of Flex Records and supported up-and-coming talent like Infernal with their bagpipe acid-trance hit "Sorti de l'Enfer" (1997). Bager was also a mentor to Remee Sigvardt Jackman, who would become an important figure in the Danish music scene as a member of Sound of Seduction, a group that further developed Cut'n'Move's blend of hip-hop and dance.

In 1996 Bager and Jan Elhøj established a suite of twenty-eight recording studios in a former industrial warehouse on

Njalsgade in Amager, a working-class neighborhood south of Copenhagen, where Aqua recorded their early demos among the likes of Los Umbrellos, Tiggy, Cartoons, Barcode Brothers, and DJ Aligator (all characters who will dip in and out of this narrative to varying degrees). I emphasize the musical and stylistic trends that Aqua shared with other late 1990s Danish Bubblegum dance acts as a means of contextualizing the elements of their music and visuals that catapulted *Aquarium* to global renown. Rather than set Aqua apart, this chapter traces *Aquarium*'s employment of Danish Bubblegum dance tropes to situate themselves in a global pop landscape, specifically the distinctive Scandinavian presence in late 1990s Japan.

The band formed amidst this rise in production two years earlier, in 1994, when René Dif met the aspiring musicians Claus Norreen and Søren Rasted. Claus and Søren began their musical collaboration at eighteen after meeting in a gas station outside of Copenhagen where Claus worked to fund his passion for New Wave records and making industrial techno. Although Claus was not necessarily a musical child, he developed a fascination with electronics and acquired his first keyboard at fourteen. Søren, on the other hand, was raised in a home where music was central: he received piano lessons from his mother beginning at age five and kept up with his training while staying with a musical family as an exchange student to the United States.

After meeting, the pair moved in together and began to compose songs. The duo found their first success in 1994, when they won a competition to compose the soundtrack for the children's film *Frække Frida og de frygtløse spioner* (Naughty

I'm a Bubblegum Girl

Frida and the Fearless Spies). The soundtrack is a mix of bouncy staccato synth music and upbeat children's vocals. When recording at Sweet Silence Studio in Amager, they realized they needed a rapper; Claus and Søren happened into the discotheque Harlequin where they found René rapping over his DJ set. They liked what they heard and brought him in for the track "Si-Bab-Rapper-Di-Åhh."

During his youth in the Copenhagen suburb of Frederiksberg, René grappled with the demands of school and his unflagging energy for exploration that often manifested as distraction and misbehavior that he now speculates were perhaps the result of an undiagnosed attention deficit disorder.[1] René was a rebellious teenager in the mid-1980s and found community when he discovered hip-hop and joined a breakdancing crew. At fifteen, he was arrested during a drink-and-dash spree across Copenhagen pubs with his friends. This run-in with the law prompted René to evaluate his decisions and, after finishing gymnasium, he joined a Danish shipping company as a sailor. While working on St. Lucia in the Caribbean, René discovered an impactful DJ on a local radio station and decided to try his hand after returning to Copenhagen. "René Dif, International DJ," as his promo photos proclaimed, had a rather humble start, first in a mobile disco and then in a small discotheque in Roskilde. He cut his teeth at clubs in Norway and Greece and became known for combining his spinning ability with a penchant for rapping.[2]

[1] René Dif, Lene Nystrøm, and Søren Rasted, "Hvem er Aqua? 1:4," Interview by Søren Bygbjerg. Hvem er? DR Lyd, September 30, 2022, Audio, 52:00, https://www.dr.dk/lyd/p3/hvem-er/hvem-er-aqua-1-4.
[2] Ibid.

I thought to be a DJ that just stood there and played records was a little bit boring. I was also break dancing from when I was very young. I was influenced by American DJs and rap music. And then I just started one day. I actually went outside the DJ booth and started rapping without knowing what people would think about it. They freaked out and thought it was cool.[3]

Working on the soundtrack together did not bring immediate success, but it solidified their creative relationship. With Claus and Søren holding down the musical foundation and René stepping forward as a vocalist, the trio began writing and recording together. Yet, they felt an element was missing and began to look for a female lead singer who could round out the group, a model drawn from the success of contemporary Eurodance groups like Cut'N'Move and La Bouche in Germany.

Enter Lene Nystrøm, the charismatic Norwegian singer with a distinctive clarion voice integral to Aqua's sound. René and Lene met while working—as a DJ and hostess, respectively—on a ferry between Oslo and Copenhagen. Lene was raised in the city of Tønsberg, Norway. Lene was drawn to the stage from a young age; she took violin lessons from a neighbor, jazz and ballet classes from the age of six, and was known for her homemade performance of pop tunes with a hairbrush microphone. She grew up listening to ABBA, Boney M, and American Rock'n'roll, but the winning Norwegian Eurovision act Bobbysocks (a 1950s-revival pop-rockabilly duo) inspired

---

[3] Andy Greene, "'People Probably Want to Kill Us': The Oral History of Aqua's 'Barbie Girl,'" *Rolling Stone*, April 1, 2022, https://www.rollingstone.com/music/music-features/aqua-barbie-girl-oral-history-1319069/.

her to sing.[4] She channeled this love for showbiz as a host for *Casino*, a Norwegian gameshow based on *Wheel of Fortune*. Although it was a silent roll, while filming her last episode Lene was unexpectedly thrust in the limelight to sing an acapella rendition of "Almaz," a touching R&B ballad popularized by Randy Crawford. The producers were so impressed that they offered Lene and the show's host a position on the cruise ship. And the rest is history. "To make a long story short," recounts René, "Lene and I went out for a few years after meeting on the boat." "He spent a couple of months flirting my pants off," Lene cheekily replied in a recent interview.[5] René learned Lene had the chops to front the band while on board; she recalls, "He was playing me some music from another project he was working on. I remember listening to another girl singing it and thinking 'I can sing better than her.' I told René and his reaction was 'Can you sing?' That was it—I was in the band!"[6]

The foursome became fast friends and began making music together. In the band's early months, Lene traveled back and forth from Norway. Ultimately, she left her job with a jeweler and relied on René to help support them both: "It sounds funny now," René remembers, "but we really lived on nothing. I was DJ-ing at the weekends and that was it." But the band was not yet Aqua as we know them today. In 1994, the small Swedish label XM signed the group under the moniker Joyspeed and in 1995 released their one and only single, "Itzy Bitzy." The track barely broke through, spending one week at number 52

---

[4] Jacqui Swift, *Aqua: The Official Book (London: Virgin Books, 1998),* 13–14.

[5] Greene, "People Probably . . ."

[6] Swift, *Aqua: The Official Book,* 13–14.

in Sweden. The original version of the reinterpreted nursery rhyme is middling; a down-tempo, reggae-inflected track with a relaxed bassline, ethereal synth harmonies, percussion mostly comprised of maracas and a hi-hat, and a vocoded femme voice that says "yeah" on syncopated beats in the background. Lene sings the first verse and occasionally adds some sensually improvisational phrasings of "itsy bitsy." René's rap verses are bizarre: the lyrics first harass the spider, "he's all that fast and he's so damn small," then sexualize the gendered arachnid "with his sexy legs and hairy back, he reach [sic] the most of people's shit." Independent of the song's kitsch puerility, the four remixes produced by the band to accompany the single laid an important foundation for Aqua's Bubblegum Eurodance sound. "Hard Radio Spider" veers from swaying reggae into the pounding bounce of happy hardcore—a high BPM subgenre of break-beat hardcore that emerged around 1994 characterized by a four-to-the-floor kick drum, arpeggiated piano rolls, uplifting and silly lyrics, simple major-key melodies, and vocals pitched up into the chipmunk range. The "K. Boff World Mix" corrects some of the original's shortcomings with Lene's naturally high-pitched voice as an "analogue" substitute for the shrill squeak common to the related Dutch genre of Gabber. Combined with the introduction of an acid synth riff that relishes the crunchy attack of a Roland-303, the final remix stands as a solid club-ready track at a brisk 190 beats per minute.

While even the group admits that it was not their best work, I underscore the significance of the "Itzy Bitzy" remixes as a precursor to *Aquarium* precisely because they are not very "good" by the rubrics of commercial success and musical erudition. The remixes work within established generic conventions while also translating aspects of hardcore into an early form of Bubblegum dance that would be palatable to adult audiences at the rave *as well as* adolescent radio listeners tuned into the lyrics. To put it simply, the remixes produce a queer camp musically without depending on the persona of the performer. This distinction points to a persistent trend in pop music scholarship, highlighted by Jodi Taylor, that relies on performative style to affirm the musical interpretation of camp queerness.[7] Musicologist Stan Hawkins's scholarship reorients these readings of queer musical camp with a method that "involves investigating the role of music technology, especially with regard to digital editing and production techniques." Nevertheless, Hawkins's analysis ultimately argues that "music furnishes camp by stylizing and complementing performances in sight as much as sound," where camp emerges from the relationship between "the surface properties of an artist's *look*" and "the musical properties of sound."[8] Without a video or promotional photography, the camp that emerges from the relationship between Joyspeed's "Itzy Bitzy" and its remixes demonstrates the capacity for music to be read as queer independent of the performer. This approach aligns with Freya Jarman-Ivens's analysis of the voice in popular music:

[7] Philip Auslander, *Performing Glam Rock: Gender and Theatricality in Popular Music* (Ann Arbor: University of Michigan Press, 2006), 150–92; Simon Frith, *Performing Rites: On the Value of Popular Music* (Cambridge: Harvard University Press, 1998), 203–25; Taylor, *Playing it Queer*, 78.

[8] Stan Hawkins, *Queerness in Pop Music: Aesthetics, Gender Norms, and Temporality* (New York: Routledge, 2016), 135–6.

Its bodily origin and destination, and its operations across borders and through borders, and its traversal of the space between bodies, collectively give the voice a physical location in two bodies and in no body at all, and its meaning arguably arises in all three locations too. . . . In gendered terms, then, the voice is a slippery beast and already potentially queer in this way.[9]

As the remixes of "Itzy Bitzy" accentuate and subtract various elements of the "original," so too do they allow for queer camp operations between and across listening publics and counter-publics.[10]

Joyspeed's campy hardcore was short-lived, however, and the band annulled their contract with XM to refine their sound. Using entry-level synthesizers and limited mixing resources, the foursome recorded a bare-bones demo that included "Barbie Girl" and "Roses Are Red," Aqua's first single from *Aquarium*. Early in 1996, the foursome found themselves in the office of Niclas Anker, an A&R (artist and repertoire) specialist at Universal Records during a moment when the Danish division almost exclusively marketed American pop music. But Anker was struck by the group's combination of musical potential and the ineffable charisma that is "star power."[11] Anker was so involved with the band during this period that he was considered a fifth member. Anker introduced the band to John Aargard, an established manager in Denmark, who offered them a contract with Universal Denmark in the summer of 1996. "We

[9] Jarman-Ivens, *Queer Voices*, 19.
[10] Michael Warner, *Publics and Counterpublics* (New York: Zone Books, 2002), 81.
[11] Niclas Anker, Interview with the author, February 4, 2022.

were so eager that we signed and sent it back straight away!" says Søren, "Then we partied our brains out!"[12]

With a contract in hand and access to a studio, the fledgling band recorded many of the demos that would comprise their debut album while their friends "were getting sunburned at the beach."[13] Having shed "Joyspeed" because it no longer suited their style, the band needed a name. "We were doing a concert in Copenhagen and we had to think of a name really quickly for the poster," recalls Lene. Søren and Claus remember that they had been tossing around ideas for some time when René phoned while heading to a DJ gig in Norway and proposed "Aquarium" based on a poster from Danmarks Akvarium that hung in the studio.[14] Sometimes the best ideas are the most straightforward, and, with a slight abbreviation, Aqua was born.

Musically, Aqua's sound changed dramatically when they serendipitously acquired a Roland JV-1080. Released in 1994, the JV-1080 was an industry-standard MIDI sound module with a range of unique sounds or "patches" and sixteen-part multitimbrality—meaning multiple patches could be played at the same time to produce a rich composition on a single keyboard. In addition, there were a number of expansion boards that could be used in conjunction with the JV-1080 to tailor the module to a specific genre. The production of *Aquarium* relied on the "Dance" Expansion Board, coveted because its distribution was curtailed due to copyright issues.

[12] Swift, *Aqua: The Official Book*, 26.
[13] *The Aqua Diary: The Official Aquarium Home Video,* directed by Peder Pedersen, 1998, Australia: Universal Music Group, 1998, VHS.
[14] Ibid.

These features amounted to a versatile synthesizer for making expansive, layered music on a single module. It had recently been supplanted by the JV-2080 making the older model a *relatively* affordable way into the music production (although the price tag of nearly £1100 was nothing to scoff at).[15] The synthesizer, now recognized as an integral component of Aqua's production, was not originally intended for the band. Anker rented the JV-1080 for another group, but they breached the contract because they did not return the module on time, forcing Anker to purchase it outright. When Søren and Claus saw it in his office, they immediately recognized a momentous opportunity and took it to the studio. "From that point on the whole sound changed," recalls Anker, a sentiment echoed across narratives of Aqua's ascent on the global stage.[16]

With the development of a signature sound under way, the newly minted Aqua turned their attention toward their public image to couch earnest musicianship within a cartoonish aesthetic. In September 1996, Aqua released their first single "Roses Are Red" to great success. It entered the Danish charts at number 14, steadily climbed to number 1 for nine weeks, and reached the top of Tjeklisten, Denmark's popular chart, where listeners wrote in to vote for their favorite hits. According to Søren, the band may have even written in a few letters of their

[15]"Roland Super JV1080: Expandable Synthesizer Module," *Sound on Sound,* December 1994, https://www.soundonsound.com/reviews/roland-super-jv 1080; Greene, "People Probably...". There is some uncertainty as to whether Aqua used a Roland JV1080 or JV2080 on the production of *Aquarium*. A recent Rolling Stone article lands on the side of the more cutting-edge model. I follow Karsten Delgado's studio equipment list from the album.
[16]Niclas Anker, Interview with the author, August 31, 2022.

own.[17] In order to introduce Aqua to a secondary market, a vinyl single with remixes was pressed on ZAC records out of Italy, where there was a taste for Eurodance from local clubbers and tourists alike.[18]

Around the time of its release, Aqua toured Denmark's discotheques every weekend playing six-song, twenty-minute sets at four or more different clubs on a Friday night. The crew ran a tight ship with one car driving ahead to set up, and another following with the band. Within the span of a few months, particularly after the release of "Roses Are Red," there were lines of people waiting to see the band and then caravans of fans following the group from venue to venue. Lene and René led the charge in developing their dynamic stage presence that was not driven by choreography (as was the case with many of their pop contemporaries) but an improvisational style driven by a flirtatious engagement with each other and the audience. Aqua put this extensive stage experience to the test on New Years' Eve 1996, when they played at Discotheque In, Copenhagen's largest, hippest club. The club owner decided to arrange for a special surprise, packing a confetti cannon full of rose petals that would rain on the audience as Aqua played their hit single. The stunt quite literally backfired, however, and, instead of a dramatic shower, the canon exploded on stage and hurled Claus and his keyboard to the ground.[19]

[17]"Hvem er Aqua? 2:4," Interview by Søren Bygbjerg. Hvem er? DR Lyd, September 30, 2022, https://www.dr.dk/lyd/p3/hvem-er/hvem-er-aqua-2-4.
[18]Anker, Interview, August 31, 2022.
[19]Søren Rasted, Interview with the author, October 10, 2022; Lene Nystrøm, Interview with the author, October 13, 2022.

Alongside extensive radio play in Scandinavia and in southern European discotheques, Aqua released a video to accompany the single. Although their budget was small, their dreams were big. They hired one of the premier advertising photographers working for Denmark's popular teen publication, *Chili Magazine*. Christian Dyekjær, a childhood friend of Søren's, directed the video, the band enlisted friends and interested Roskilde festival goers to participate, and the band's parents made sandwiches for the crew. The video cuts between two scenes: in one, Aqua performs alone on a white soundstage with a burgundy couch and vintage electric organ for props. The other is a *Revenge of the Nerds*-style party where identically dressed male wallflowers awkwardly stand together until Aqua's music and copious amounts of beer inspire them to let loose and dance with throngs of beautiful women before passing out in the aftermath (Figure 2).

As the video circulated, *Aquarium* was released on March 26, 1997. With the album ascending charts across the globe,

Figure 2 *Still from Aqua's "Roses Are Red," screengrab by the author.*

Aqua began performing outside of Denmark for the first time (apart from a few dates in neighboring Norway) and embarked on an eighteen-month-long world tour that started in Japan. Where "My Oh My" spelled Aqua's fame in Scandinavia and "Barbie Girl" in most of the rest of the world, "Roses Are Red" was their biggest hit in Japan. The band also remembers their renown in Japan as a surprise, "It was such a big thing!" Lene recalls, "The fans were so loud—they were screaming continuously. We couldn't believe it because we didn't think we were that popular at the time." Claus characterized the scene at a club in Nagoya as "a mad flip out. We arrived and there was water running down the walls because there were so many people there."[20] Aqua's popularity in Nagoya can in part be attributed to their frequent play on the radio station Zip-FM, which held important sway because of its listener base in a city that predominately commuted by car, unlike all other major metro areas in Japan.[21]

Aqua's acclaim in Japan was not an isolated occurrence and benefits from an elaboration on the unexpected popularity of Scandinavian dance music in the late 1990s. The cross-cultural appeal was clear by April of 1997, when Charles Ferro reported, "Danish music is making deep inroads into export markets around the world particularly in Japan and the Far East. Industry executives have attempted to explain the success by citing a long tradition of melodious Scandinavian folk music, but what it really boils down to is hard work promoting catchy songs." And no one was more invested in

---

[20] Swift, *Aqua: The Official Book*, 18–19.
[21] Tatsu Nakamoto, Interview with the author, February 15, 2022.

the hard work of promotion than Aqua's marketing manager Niclas Anker, who echoed Ferro's assessment, "The whole of Asia is flipping over Scandinavian music."[22] Universal Victor, the Japanese arm of Universal Records, was instrumental in introducing Scandinavian Bubblegum dance through Tatsuya Nakamoto, the product manager for all non-US music in Japan. Nakamoto's first major success was the introduction of the Swedish chanteuse Pandora, best known for her 1993 Hi-NRG hit "Trust Me." After meeting with Universal Denmark employees in 1996, including John Aagaard, Niclas Anker, and Jens-Otto Paludan, Nakamoto applied a similar set of marketing strategies to Aqua.

Beyond Universal Japan, a surprising number of Scandinavian dance-pop crossover acts found success in the Japanese market because of their inclusion on the twenty-two *Dancemania* compilations released by EMI. Many of these high-energy tracks were then featured in the innovative kinetic video game *Dance Dance Revolution* (DDR) because EMI controlled licensing rights to the Danish Bubblegum dance acts Ni-Ni, Me & My, Papaya, and multiple tracks from Smile.dk who contributed "Butterfly," perhaps the most famous song from the franchise. These tracks share a taste for bright and bubbly feminine vocals that sweeten the metronomically pounding 4/4 beat. Devoid of any swing, the impeccable regularity of these songs is perfect for a videogame where points are scored by executing increasingly complex step patterns on beat.

---

[22] Charles Ferro, "Danish Delight in Eastern Promise," *Music and Media* 14, no. 18 (May 3, 1997): 16.

In addition to these musical similarities, the Danish Bubblegum dance tracks featured on DDR emblematize the genre's knack for hooking the listener with the irresistible simplicity of their lyrics that are almost ancillary to the track itself. Like the non-lexical vocables of Me & My's "Dub-i-Dub," the song "1, 2, 3, 4, 007" by Ni-Ni (Nynne Qvortrup) diminishes meaning in favor of melody with a chorus of non-sequential counting employed for the sake of rhyme: "1, 2, 3, 4, 007, All the good guys go to heaven, 5, 6, 7, 8, hey, hey! All the rest can go away." Sure, the two verses clue the listener into Ni-Ni's struggle to find the perfect man, but the real star is the chorus, repeated six times in under four minutes, that promises to wedge its way into the deepest part of your psyche. With Ni-Ni as a paradigmatic case, the lyrics of Danish Bubblegum dance tracks achieve a minimum threshold of "meaningful" signification for the listener to hold onto. They are reminiscent of nursery rhymes, using nonsensical phrases to reinforce a moral lesson with rhyme and melody.

It is obvious, but important, to state that in global pop contexts where English is not the first language, focus is often placed on the song's ability to hook the listener by concocting a balance between catchy melodies and lyrics that unambiguously capture emotions in ways translatable beyond a singular national or linguistic context. Reflecting on Denmark's international success in 1998, Sony Denmark A&R manager Poul Martin Bonde speculates, "It's the melodies. We have a strong tradition of folk nursery rhymes with catchy tunes."[23] Tatsuya Nakamoto confirms this, emphasizing that

[23] Gary Smith, "Danish 'tackno' Brings Home the Bacon," *Music and Media* 15, no. 15 (April 11, 1998): 7.

the appeal of Aqua was in part due to their ability to craft refrains that were easy to remember, particularly when they sounded like Japanese phrases, and especially for audiences who would be new to learning English, those around ten to fourteen.[24]

But was Aqua producing music for the age group now generally known as "tweens"? With Joyspeed's "Itzy Bitzy" and "Roses Are Red" at the fore, Aqua fits nicely within the group of Danish artists making music for DDR: clichéd lyrics set to a high-energy beat that could hold even the most distractible adolescent's attention. In his recent study *Tween Pop*, media scholar Tyler Bickford argues the tween—defined as "a demographic label that became widespread in the 1990s to consolidate an awkward but profitable marketing category of nine- to twelve-year-olds"—emerged as a discrete consumer in the American music industry after the turn of the millennium with the release of *Kidz Bop 1*.[25] Rather, millennial tween music "went out of its way to fit fully within the conventions of mainstream pop, and did as little as possible to clean up those conventions—so while lyrics downplayed physical sex, they were still full of heterosexual romance, pop music's central subject."[26] Contextualizing the immense popularity of "Roses Are Red" within the broader ecosystem of Danish Bubblegum dance in Japanese media culture suggests that a type of tween pop music culture had already coalesced outside of anglophone markets in the late 1990s, influenced by the global ubiquity of American media. In the Scandinavian

---

[24]Nakamoto, Interview with the author, February 15, 2022.
[25]Tyler Bickford, *Tween Pop* (Durham: Duke University Press, 2020), 4, 41–55.
[26]Ibid., 19.

context, media scholar Ingvild Kvale Sørenssen has traced the in-betweenness of the tween in her studies of Norwegian adolescents' engagement with Disney products and *High School Musical*'s role in the construction of the category.[27]

But Aqua's songs are not just for kids, they straddle the juvenile and adult with themes about love and sexual inuendo thinly veiled behind jejune metaphors of animals, superheroes, toys, and the like. The group did not conform to Bickford's early 2000s account of pop songs "cleaned up" to America's prudish standards for tween audiences. With a song like "Roses Are Red," the queer camp punchline lies in the fact that it begins with inuendo, but flirtatiously flips the intensity so that what would be erotic subtext in other Bubblegum dance tracks is laid bare. A rush of wind and a sharp vibrato synth chord set the mood as Lene enters with the crisp articulation of the nursery rhyme—"Roses are red, and violets are blue, honey is sweet, but not as sweet as you"—accompanied by a piano melody. She repeats the first couplet, but a reversed recording of Lene singing the bridge replaces the second half of the verse. The switch flips and the mood shifts, with Lene repeating "Dum-de-da-di-dum" as a snare drum roll and bassline crescendo underneath. Suddenly, the bass cuts; René's husky voice exclaims, "Come pick my roses"; and the listener is thrown into kiddy clubland with a pulsing four-to-the-floor kick and the phased warble of

[27]Ingvild Kvale Sørenssen, "Domesticating the Disney Tween Machine: Norwegian Tweens Enacting Age and Everyday Life" (PhD diss., Norwegian University of Science and Technology, 2014); Ingvild Kvale Sørenssen, "Disney's *High School Musical* and the Construction of the Tween Audience," *Global Studies of Childhood* 8, no. 3 (September 2018): 213–24.

a second synth hook. Now the lyrics play with the inuendo of the original poem to proclaim Lene's orgasmic desire: "Sweet from the flowers, honey from the bees, I've got a feeling, I'm ready to release." René reenters, establishing the back-and-forth role play common to many songs on *Aquarium*, singing about cupid's immaterial pull into eros, something "invisible, but, so touchable," something he can "feel on [his] body, so emotional," making him a "victim of a hot love messenger." Lene turns up the heat beckoning her partner to "show it to me truly, show it with a kiss." The song devolves into repetitions of "dum-de-da-di-dum" which now seem closer to the vocalizations of sensual pleasure than a puerile melody for children. The recontextualized repetition of these non-lexical elements provides a coy reminder that, like "Itzy Bitzy," this may be a nursery rhyme, but it is one retooled for a night of physical proximity in the club.

The precocious flirtation of "Roses Are Red," reinforced through infectious redundancy, demonstrates Aqua's innovations to Danish Bubblegum dance and distinguishes its ability to employ camp to traverse genres from other continental Eurodance ventures in the mid-1990s. For instance, it has no designs on the earnest pop-dance of Ace of Base, whose 1995 release *The Bridge* contains the cloyingly optimistic "Beautiful Life" alongside the stalwart, dub-inflected beat of "Never Going to Say I'm Sorry." Nor does it lean into the hypersexual absurdity of Eurobeat group E-Rotic, whose high-NRG single "Max don't have sex with your ex" adopts a near limerick rhyme scheme to warn against a sexual escapade that "will make your life complex." Aqua's first single picks up certain threads from both strains and adds a ludic quality that allows childish innuendo to open onto the uninhibited space of the dancefloor.

Søren offers a related but different entry point to this question of lyrical profundity. He describes lyrics not as the driving force of a song but the means to give meaning to a fantastical sonic universe that was not necessarily "heavy" nor connected to lived experiences.[28] From one perspective (most frequently a native anglophone one), the presumed lack of "depth" can be construed as a derision of other international English-es seen as charming or quaint because the syntax is not flawless, or an unintended connotation intrudes on otherwise correct denotation. This vantage produces the perception of "Europop" as schlocky, trite, or fatuous because of its lyrical simplicity. From another vantage, these songs astutely manipulate a shared vocabulary to distill experiences shared across global manifestations of late stage capitalism. While these everyday escapades—love and loss, the desire for material accumulation, the quotidian grind of a job, or even more ineffable feelings like joy and sadness—certainly have unique expressions in specific cultural contexts, global pop succeeds when it proves relatable across them. There exists, however, a third, queer relation between these two poles driven by the ironic reverence of camp. The queer listener— and, more specifically, *this* anglophone queer listener—hears in the expanse between these two poles. There is certainly a helping of cheesiness in this genre, but does that not make it even more impressive when a track manages to elicit a chuckle while tugging at your heartstrings? Yes, the squelching bass

---

[28] Søren Rasted, Interview with the author, October 10, 2022.

run and opening "dub-i-dub-i-dub-dub-dub" of Me & My's hit are ridiculous in their flatulent drama—as were Whigfield's quacking ducks three years prior. Yet abandoning "good taste" also adds texture to the anthemic harmonies proclaiming the end of a relationship with a negligent lover who has come crawling back.

Taking this from pop radio into the queer club (or living room) allows other forms of social defiance to be heard. As Moe Meyer argues, queer camp becomes the means for disenfranchised readers to advance their own interests by creating new codes that cohere around pre-existing forms of cultural discourse.[29]

In this case, the signifying opportunities offered by the relationship between lexical and non-lexical elements in songs like "Dub-i-Dub" and "Roses Are Red" open a capacious queer ground from which might spring a parody of the very heteronormative that is the ostensible subject of the song.

In their interpretation of the song, queer Copenhagen artists peachlyfe (Petra Skibsted, a pioneer in Denmark's speed techno scene), KimKim (Kim Mejdahl, a queer visual and performance artist), and Proxy Server (a multi-media queer performance artist) strip down the silliness of Aqua's original—with its warbling organ melody, the inordinate formality in Lene's elongated pronunciation, and René's emphatic delivery. They produce a slick and paired-back dancefloor heater that could warm even a seasoned Berlin raver. A full minute and a half longer than the original, the rework is closer to the

[29] Moe Meyer, "Reclaiming the Discourse of Camp," in *The Poetics and Politics of Camp*, ed. Moe Meyer (London: Routledge, 1994), 1–20.

I'm a *Bubblegum* Girl

song's remixes and structurally insists on its proximity to the dancefloor. The cover's stomping solemnity queerly reorients Aqua's brazenly self-conscious kitsch toward a camp that feigns seriousness while simultaneously undermining it. It opens with a single staccato melody line and a feminine vocoder voice recites the titular poem like an attentive schoolchild before the kick drum starts to pound a four-four and KimKim breathily delivers an invitation for the listener to "come pick my roses." Proxy Server maintains the sultry energy of the rework in their delivery of the verse, yet the alien-ness of the auto-tune brings the listener into a fantasized proximity predicated on the queerness of the unknown rather than the presumption of knowing.[30]

The rest of the verse is sung in Danish and shifts the lyrics slightly to disentangle desire from a singular lover; here "*honning er sød, men ikke lige så sød (som dig)*." The comparison is refused, answered only by the vagaries of René's verse sung by KimKim where the "it" that is "so touchable" remains undefined. KimKim's aloof rasp also shifts some of the lyrics from English to Danish, "*kom og pluk min roser*." At one level, these linguistic shifts call back to Aqua as a Danish-Norwegian band. On another, they challenge the assumption that the easily

---

[30] Catherine Provenzano, "Making Voices: The Gendering of Pitch Correction and the Auto-Tune Effect in Contemporary Pop Music," Journal of Popular Music Studies 31:2 (June 2019): 63–84. In her article, Provenzano points to the limitations auto-tune imposes on women in pop music because of its associations with deskilling and obfuscating the "authenticity of the voice." She does not, however, fully account for auto-tune as a generative form of gendered vocality for trans performers. My discussion of auto-tune and other digital vocal modifications here, and throughout this book, attempts to contribute to trans-feminine approaches to the voice in pop and electronic music.

comprehensible English lyrics are the point of intersection between global appeal and a camp interpretation. Instead, these three queer Copenhageners camp the seemingly serious sensuality of Aqua's debut outside of a singular linguistic register and in the affective register of the music itself. One need not speak Danish, but perhaps must speak queer camp, to understand the coy refusal of Proxy Server's incomplete comparison, the allure of KimKim's repeated dare to "come on," and the elements of 1990s trance (so often dismissed as saccharine) in the instrumentation that peachlyfe brings into the twenty-first century. By nearly inverting the tone of the original, this collaborative rework draws out the camp that resides in the extra-linguistic elements of music, where a camp performance of nursery rhyme adaptation of a Spencerian love poem becomes a space of queer play. If one does not just read between the lines but inverts them all together—as the rework inverts the placement of Lene's vocals run backwards from the beginning to the end of the song—one can coopt heteronormative clichés of desire to queer ends, with a wink of course.

2   I'm a *Baroque* Girl

"Roses are Red" was still on the Danish charts in February 1997 when "My Oh My" was released as the second Danish single from the forthcoming album. In a feature for *Billboard* later in the year Anker noted: "It's the first time in around 20 years that one artist has had two hits in the [Danish] top 10 at the same time."[1]

After the release of their first single and with a video under their belt, Aqua retreated to Gjøl, a northern Danish town of 200 people, in the winter of 1996–7 to record (Figure 3). During this period the band adapted techniques from other successful Eurodance bands while also innovating the genre. Claus and Søren wrote all their songs, blending club-forward dance with the verse-chorus structure and hooky lyrics of pop. With an ear for this unique crossover sound, Aqua produced a compelling debut album with tracks spanning infectious earworms, Latin-inflected summer jams, and schmaltzy ballads. *Aquarium*'s extensive play in clubs and on the radio was, to a certain extent, guided by the album's producers, Karsten Delgado and Johnny Jam, who came to the project with extensive experience in Denmark's rave and underground radio scene. The album achieved a remarkable balance where instrumentation and vocals dance above, within, and around

---

[1] Charles Ferro, "Global Music Pulse, Denmark," *Billboard*, March 29, 1997, 53.

Figure 3 *Lene and René in the vocal booth, photography from 1996 to 1997, reproduced from the collection of Karsten Delgado.*

the synthesizers colored by Mackie mixers. Delgado and Jam's deft "crossover" approach that blended live recording with electronic elements central to genres like techno, house, and acid resulted in a lush soundscape where the intersecting percussion, bass, and melody lines create an almost baroque intricacy.[2]

"My Oh My" was the first release to reflect Aqua's developed sound and cultivated image that would take the world by storm in 1997. Trotting hooves slowly crescendo for two measures before they are connected to a horse's whinny. This rhythmic triplet, composed with a sample of coconuts (à la *Monty Python and the Holy Grail* according to Delgado), exists out of the present and in an indefinite pre-modern past. Then enters the unmistakably sharp pluck of a synthesized

Aqua's Aquarium

---

[2] Karsten Delgado, Interview with the author, February 11, 2022.

spinet—a smaller version of the harpsicord developed in the seventeenth century. With a remarkable economy of instrumentation, "My Oh My" holds the listener between two dancefloors, one in the synthesized now and the other in the Baroque then. Lene adds her voice to the composition with the staid exclamation "My oh my," followed by "do you want to say goodbye?" and then a solidification of our vaguely specific temporal location, "to have a kingdom baby, tell me why . . . to rule a country, baby, you and I?" A virtuosic spinet run builds suspense and introduces the bassline that cycles through a movement up a minor third, down a major third, up a perfect fourth, a triplet on the major second, and completes the cycle by moving down a minor third.

The bassline employs the song's distinctly emotional minor key to play up the lyrical narrative of pining love incongruous against the lush and shiny instrumentation. Claus and Søren used the minor key to create compelling and intriguing pop by playing the key's sadness against the energetic positivity cultivated by dance music's rapid rhythm and upbeat tempo. While the intensity of sadness experienced while listening to music in a minor key is subjective, the affective pull of these keys toward the depressive is undeniable.[3] The use of D minor for "My Oh My," however, is a particularly interesting choice. D minor has been described as "the heartbreak key," with a reputation for being "the saddest of all keys . . . it makes people

[3] Tik-Sze Carrey Siu and Him Cheung, "Infants' Sensitivity to Emotion in Music and Emotion-Action Understanding," *PLoS One* 12, no. 2 (2017), https://journals.plos.org/plosone/article?id=10.1371/journal.pone.0171023; Elizabeth Nawrot, "The Perception of Emotional Expression in Music: Evidence from Infants, Children and Adults," *Psychology of Music* 31, no. 1 (2003): 75–92.

I'm a Baroque Girl

39

weep instantly when you play it," to quote the protagonist of the 1984 mockumentary *Spinal Tap*. While D minor may not be the "saddest" key, it is often avoided in contemporary pop music. In addition to its emotional intensity, D minor may also be less frequented in pop music because it is challenging to build suspense with its chord structure. In a minor key, the third interval is flatted, lowered one-half step, thereby making it closer to the root note and creating a loose dissonance that may start to explain the downward feeling these chords inspire.

D minor chord progressions pose compositional challenges because a movement across chords tends to follow one of two paths: to one side, the listener remains stuck in the mire of sadness as opposed to a typical pop chord progression that, as Wilson characterizes it, "follows a structure of suspense and resolution."[4] Conversely, residing in the persistent gloom of D minor often pushes songwriters to counter this affective negativity with musical and lyrical irony. "My Oh My" takes the latter route, with staccato bowed violin harmonies, the bright twang of the spinet, and hissing, hi-hat-heavy percussion that floats above.

"My Oh My" takes the musical irony used to counter the sadness of its key and does it one better, inflecting it with the camp artifice of its faux-Baroque trappings. Most certainly unbeknownst to the band themselves, their decision to ironically structure the song around Baroque tropes in D minor

[4] Kat Wilson, "The Heartbreak Key: D Minor Plays On Our Rawest Emotion—But in Contemporary Music, Even the Most Somber of Artists Tend to Avoid It," *Rolling Stone*, August 18, 2021, https://www.rollingstone.com/pro/features/music-d-minor-saddest-key-1210591/.

reflects historical conceptions of the key. In his 1784 treatise *Ideas for an Aesthetic of Musical Art*, the German composer Christian Schubart described D minor and its enharmonic equivalent E flat minor as tied to "melancholic womanliness," and inspired "feelings of disquietude, of the soul's deepest urge, of brooding despair, of blackest depression, of the gloomiest condition of the soul. Every fear, every hesitation of the shuddering heart, breathes out of E flat minor. If ghosts could speak, their speech would approximate this key."[5] Returning to the verses of the song itself reveals the surprising extent to which Aqua's Eurodance romp aligns with Schubart's reflection on the affects of musical keys from the apex of both Baroque musical production and oceanic piracy.

Lene continues, in illeism, to introduce herself as a "little princess in a terrible mess," a lone monarch without someone to love despite "dreams of a prince on a tall white horse" who will sweep her off her feet from within the castle walls. Like a Bach counterpoint, René's throaty growl drops in: "Gotta steal from the rich, when they don't know I'm comin', Gotta give to the poor, no time for lovin'." In an unexpected twist of fate, the Robinhood bad boy mockingly rebuffs the princess "My oh my, don't you cry 'cause there's no way I'm stayin', I will leave say "bye bye," I'm going my way." Princess Lene is not assuaged, however.

The bass cuts to signal the introduction of what Søren calls the "energy hook," a compositional technique used throughout

[5] Christian Fredrich Daniel Schubart, *Ideen zu einer Ästhetik der Tonkunst* (Vienna: J.V. Degen, 1806), 375–6; quoted in Rita Steblin, *A History of Key Characteristics in the Eighteenth and Early-Nineteenth Centuries* (Ann Arbor: UMI Research Press, 1983), 243–4.

Aquarium that he developed with Claus. In this structure, the first "hook" is augmented or alternated with a second, more intense melody that holds the listener's interest.[6] Here, it flows into a repetition of the chorus before her second verse returns to a soliloquizing mode. The "mystery" of whether or not she can pin down her outlaw lover is seated "deep in the royal heart," making her "cry at night" and "want to be apart"—an apparent bluff for the sake of rhyme before her wedding fantasy peters out in the final chorus. In a camp twist, the "melancholic womanliness" that Schubart attributed to the key of D minor in the eighteenth century is sublimated in the ironically peppy instrumentation of "My Oh My" only to be foregrounded in the song's narrative.

Dressed in a synthesized parody of the Baroque, "My Oh My" presses against the limits of Sontag's assertion that "so many of the objects prized by Camp taste are old fashioned, out of date, *démodé*" because their distance from the conditions of the present affords more ready access to the excesses of fantasy. For Sontag, a backward glance is an integral criteria of camp because "it may enhance what seems simply dogged or lacking fantasy now because we are too close to it, because it too closely resembles our own everyday fantasies."[7] In this formulation, fantasy furnishes an aesthetic rubric to distinguish good-bad camp from the just-bad. In its psychoanalytic sense, fantasy replaces mental anguish with pleasure by constructing imaginary sequences predicated on the illusory fulfillment of a wish and are always, to a greater or lesser

---

[6] Søren Rasted, Interview with the author, October 10, 2022.
[7] Sontag, "Notes on Camp," 285.

extent, distorted from reality.[8] Thus, by looking backward in time, camp can displace the psychic stress of the present by investing this harmful surplus in a cultural object previously overlooked, dismissed, or denigrated because it was somehow aesthetically excessive in its own right when it was produced. The temporality of Sontag's camp bolsters her claim to the sensibility as "disengaged, depoliticized—or at least apolitical" because it abandons the present to escape into a fantasy of the past that latches onto a selective set of aesthetic elements divorced from their original context.[9]

It is certainly plausible to read this disengagement from the present into "My Oh My," a song made for the already-escapist space of the dancefloor that couches the tried-and-true narrative of unrequited love in a pre-modern world of pirates and chamber music. However, when appropriated for queer purposes, Aqua's second single participates in an expanded field of camp aesthetics that does not only incorporate through retroactive fantasy. As Moe Meyer argues, "dominant (read Pop) formations of camp translate [appropriation] into a recognition that Camp *was once* a homosexual discourse," situating these signifying practices "in the historical past creates the impression that the objects of camp no longer have owners and are up for grabs." For Meyer, Pop camp aligns with Sontag's depoliticized sensibility because the presumed harmlessness of objectivity erases camp's queer foundation. Thereby it "conceals a contemporaneous struggle over meanings and value

[8]Sigmund Freud, *Beyond the Pleasure Principle*, trans. James Strachey (London: Hogarth Press, 1950), 28.
[9]Sontag, "Notes on Camp," 277.

production by competing discourses."[10] True camp (that is, queer camp) retains a political valence because "the queer knows his/her signifying practices will be, *must* be appropriated."[11] In the case of "My Oh My," the competing discourses identified in Meyer's polemical reclamation camp dissolve the distinction between Pop camp and (queer) camp. The lyrics' old-fashionedness already issue a knowing glance to the listener, appropriating a queer engagement with straight romance to poke fun at itself. Yet this tawdry garb has holes, and the lyrics undo their queer critique of compulsory heterosexuality by symbolically reinforcing proto-capitalist landholding through a ludic version of the Baroque. Another few layers must be peeled back before queer can modify Pop camp in this case.

Woven into the exaggerated naïveté and heteronormative romance of the lyrics, there is a jocular layer of musical self-awareness in the spinet synth that plays with its incorporation of the out of date and *démodé* as central to its aesthetic appeal. The relationship between the seventeenth-century instrument and the loose early modern theme of the lyrics is obvious, but Aqua's use of the spinet synth adds additional camp valences because it was an unusual choice for a pop song. To achieve a new and novel sound that would stand out in a field where access to the same tools was becoming more common, Søren and Claus made the unusual choice to evoke a simulacrum of the old when writing "My Oh My."[12]

---

[10] Meyer, "Reclaiming the Discourse of Camp," 15.

[11] Ibid., 17.

[12] Valerie Doré's *The Legend* (1986) is a notable exception; an earnest Italo disco foray into the medieval with pseudo-troubadour style tracks like "The Wizard" and "Guinnevere."

Comparatively, Aqua's use of the spinet successfully balances its role as a supplement to lyrical Baroque fantasy and as a musical foundation that projects and recedes throughout the song to play with contemporary dance elements. Moreover, any illusion of sincere engagement with the past dissolves when the spinet is paired with synthesized violin flourishes, coconut clip-clopping, and the distant neighing of a horse. The spinet is camp because of its self-aware deployment, not in spite of it.

Aqua's search for a distinctive, unexpected sound in the corners of the patch library that bordered on comical has a surprising precedent in the first bars of Whigfield's pathbreaking hit. Even before her iconic "Dee dee na-na-na," "Saturday Night" sets itself apart by laying the track's foundation with a synth patch that would not register as usable for most producers: a flat quacking sound that ticks the beat for the entire song. Combined with the bassline's goofy squish, Whigfield's producers deftly incorporated sonic elements that would make the track unmistakable in a pop market where variations on a successful theme remain *de rigeur*. While not a direct citation in "My Oh My," Søren referenced Whigfield when discussing Danish producers' incorporation of synth patches that were weird or unpopular on the mainstream international scene in the 1990s.[13] One might also attribute some of Denmark's unexpected success with pop-dance crossovers to a camp sensibility that proliferated at this moment. Or, more nuanced still, the unintentionally collective choice among Danish producers to look outside of conventional instrumentation

---

[13] Søren Rasted, Interview with the author, October 10, 2022.

lent itself to camp in the 1990s and allows it to live beyond the short shelf life imposed by the industry.

The proclivity for unconventional, kitsch instrumentation among Danish dance producers meant that Aqua was not the only group to find the spinet synth lying in wait. Among them, Tiggy's "Ring A Ling" furnishes an example of the spinet in Danish Bubblegum dance most akin to Aqua's "My Oh My." They were released within months of one another and shared the conjoined formal and metaphorical use of the patch. Tiggy was the stage name of the vocalist Charlotte Vigel and was produced by Peter Hartmann and Jan Langhoff, who also worked with Aqua. In Tiggy's debut single from 1996, the spinet synth, deployed at the top of the song, piques the listener's curiosity. Christian Møller Nielsen, who would continue his career as part of the trance duo Barcode Brothers, remembers developing some of the initial elements of "Ring A Ling" after having the idea to find a place for the spinet's "medieval" sound in contemporary music.[14] Compared to the cinematic build of "My Oh My," "Ring A Ling" begins in medias res as Tiggy personifies the telephone she also uses with the onomatopoeia "Ring-a-ling, a-ling ding dong," that precedes a request to the listener who takes on the role of operator "please connect me to Prince Charming." Tiggy-as-telephone rings again as she is patched through to the Prince, or at least his voicemail, who she then commands, "be my hero be my knight. . . . I can't wait to hold you tight." "Ring A Ling" presents medieval chivalry as a saccharine metaphor for modern romance with the arpeggiated spinet line ornamented by a

---

[14] *Vild Med Dance*, Episode 3, "Pornostjerner i poolen," *DR* (June 19, 2021).

maraca shake and enveloped by the driving dance bassline. The verses use cliché medieval signifiers as a cross-temporal metaphor for feminine submission to an absent masculine suitor. She pines for him to arrive when "there will be no more pretend, I surrender to you."

The lyrical parallels to Lene's pleas for her outlaw lover in "My Oh My" are undeniable. The two tracks also share an affective melancholy hidden within a dance beat because both are written in D minor. The abundant formal and thematic similarities between these two Danish Bubblegum dance tracks afford the opportunity to home in on what might distinguish Aqua's instantiation of camp aesthetics from Tiggy's. Both employ an out-of-date historicity—at once lyrical and musical—to offer a resolution to the parodic incongruity between a hyperbolized vision of heteronormative feminine longing indexed by the pre-modern that would also get bodies moving on the dancefloor. However, where "My Oh My" offers inroads for mis-/rereading the princess's entreaties in the playful irony of camp reversal, there is an anxious urgency to Tiggy's piercing assuredness in her desire to unquestioningly surrender to her knight. The heart-wrenching D minor key that undergirds the instrumentation and lyrics heightens this overwrought heterosexuality through the generalized evocation of "the medieval." Despite the abundant similarities, Tiggy's "Ring A Ling" resides in the blissful unawareness of kitsch while Aqua's track is lined with a cheeky self-awareness that pushes into camp.

Released in 1996 ahead of *Fairytails*, her first album on Flex Records, Tiggy's debut presented her as a singular character rather than a mutable personality who could chameleon a range of pop archetypes while retaining some essence of the star beneath the mask. The entirety of *Fairytales* conflated Tiggy with a fantasized medieval princess searching, waiting, pining, and pleading for her lover. Filtered through a pulsing dance beat, Tiggy embodied a girl's ideal of a princess that could appeal to the proto-tween and dance markets. The conflation of vocalist and persona shackled Tiggy to the gender essentialism of a woman whose future is passively predicated on a male suitor—in fact, one track on the album is simply called "Waiting"—because her femininity was further limited to her "temporal drag."[15]

The video accompanying "Ring A Ling" contributes to the unified vision of Tiggy by evoking the warriors, crusaders, and a prince charming that populate the album. However, it does so in ways that make these signifiers more symbolic than literal. Presenting a fully-realized, musically and visually cohesive concept was an integral piece of the Danish Bubblegum dance puzzle. "A big part of the mid-1990s was conceptualization," remembers Kenneth Bager where the "visual expression" could be brought together with a "fantastic club number."[16] For Tiggy's hit single, this meant constructing a medieval world inflected with a late 1990s hip factor. The majority of the video focuses on Tiggy, with close-up shots of her head decked in a tawdry diadem to accent her highlighted blond hair (Figure 4). These budget simulacra of aristocratic wealth attain their full kitsch potential when the camera zooms out to reveal historical incongruities with Tiggy's costuming in

[15] Elizabeth Freeman, *Time Binds: Queer Temporalities, Queer Histories* (Durham: Duke University Press, 2010), 59–94.
[16] Vild Med Dance, Episode 3, "Pornostjerner i poolen," DR (June 19, 2021).

Figure 4 *Still Tiggy's "Ring A Ling," screengrab by author.*

late 1990s looks ornamented by aristocratic costume jewelry. For all of its low-budget, heavy-handed "Ren Faire" aesthetics, the earnest kitsch in the video for "Ring A Ling" successfully conjoined Tiggy the contemporary performer to her medieval persona, whether that be literally (Tiggy is a princess looking for love) or metaphorically (Tiggy-as-princess embodies contemporary girls' desires).

This Danish approach to pop music production should sound familiar because this was precisely the strategy employed by Aqua and their team at Universal when they were making moves to break through with "My Oh My." What distinguishes Aqua's "concept" from other Danish Bubblegum dance acts is its capacity to exist as both singularly identifiable and mutable. The video for "My Oh My," directed by Peter Stenbæk and Peder Pedersen who developed Aqua's unmistakable visual identity in image and videos, marked an important shift in the rapport between sound and image when presenting Aqua as a crossover dance-pop act with global appeal. While most of

Aqua's videos were released alongside the singles—following the industry standard—"My Oh My" is a unique case because the single and its video were not released together. Rather, the video was the last from *Aquarium*, filmed during the summer of 1998 after the band had achieved global stardom and was gearing up for the sophomore album.

The video for "My Oh My" opens by translating the clopping of coconut hooves into a galloping horse marionette that fades to a panning shot of a tenebrous music room lit by candelabras with glasses and decanters of mysteriously bright blue and green liquids. A shadowy figure in a tricorne hat and leather vest plays a harpsichord (close enough to a spinet) with his back to the camera. A heavy-handed side wipe ushers Lene into the scene from the left where she approaches a window dressed in a silk robe that slides off her shoulder as she begins to sing the first chorus. When Lene announces that her lover might have a "kingdom," a small, double-exposed circular vignette of a hand opening a chest of gold and jewels metonymically links love and property to specie before the scene dissolves again to comically deliver the punchline: René plays the harpsichord with one hook for a hand. Here the prelude veers away from the song's narrative as the flunky pirates Claus and Søren, dressed in dirty, tattered tunics, emerge from the shadows of Lene's bedchamber and kidnap her. Although there is little, if any, reference to piracy in the lyrics, Stenbæk and Pedersen homed in on an instantly recognizable "pre-modern" pastiche of visual conventions well established by Hollywood.

The eruption of the "energy hook" signals the narrative start of the music video, the title written in a Gothic script undulates like a sail catching wind against establishing shots of the ship, sepia-toned portraits of Aqua's nautical characters are printed on aged sheets of paper. A first-person, eye-level shot resumes the movement of the plot as the burlap sack is removed from the camera lens to an extreme close-up of Søren, his ruddy face twisted in a menacing laugh with mouth agape revealing teeth hastily blacked out, as Claus irreverently cackles in the background. A reverse angle shot reveals our perspective is Lene's, bound to the mast in a perfectly pink dress and tiara that stands out against her bright-red bangs. She recoils from her captors, who seem more buffoon than pirate. They produce an ironic discrepancy between Lene's expressed fear of sexual violence and their physical comedy of contorted, grimacing faces supplemented with diagetic sound effects. René's exaggerated jerking movements, produced in part by his peg leg and hook hand, present the image of an inept captain who inadvertently cuts a sheet that releases a block that collides with his skull, much to Lene's delight.

As the scene shifts with the transition from verse to chorus, Lene has been repositioned from the mast to another beam, her wrists cross tied in front of her such that they are aligned with her face in the foreground (Figure 5). Lene is exposed to the three pirates behind her; Claus wields a whip that repeatedly cracks against her back while René and Søren giddily take great joy in the scene of torture, so much so that René lifts his patch and crosses his eyes to get a better look. The dynamic of hapless abductors and fearful abductee veers onto the precipice between camp BDSM and misogynist abuse. The evocation of kink in the video for "My Oh My" is indicative of Aqua's propensity to

Figure 5 *Still from Aqua's "My Oh My," screengrab by the author.*

flirt with sexual taboo throughout their videos in the form of comical, and debatably parodic, enactments. This scene is shot from a slightly elevated vantage point and arranged along a diagonal with the close-up of Lene's bust and tied wrists occupying half the frame. She sings the first half of the chorus directly to the viewer, breaking the fourth wall to give a full view of her expression drained of fear and replaced by seductive smiles of pleasure that follow the tension and relaxation that accompany each lash.

Feminine gender exploration with fetish bondage has a long history in pop music with, for example, the Eurythmics' gender-bending power dynamics in "Sweet Dreams," Madonna's scandalous exploration of leather in "Erotica," and Rhianna's colorful assertion of Black femme pleasure as a dom in "S&M."[17] Unlike these BDSM-forward tracks that translate feminist kink into popular culture, Aqua's foray into whips and chains operates in a gray area of uneven gendered power dynamics where Lene's coerced captivity appears to melt in

---

[17] Geffen, *Glitter Up the Dark*, 114–39.

the face of pleasure as she submits to the alluring pain of the whip wielded by her male captors. Reflecting on the video's cheeky portrayal of BDSM, Lene remarks that there is

> always a sexual undertone in the lyrics and especially in the videos. In "My Oh My," for example, I'm being whipped by all of [the other members] and totally liking it while I'm looking into the camera in orgasmic singing on. I'm not sure that would go well today; it was problematic at that time, in a sense: Are they for children or are they for grownups?

She goes on to say that they never intentionally targeted a single age demographic, although some of the sexual "undertones" are in fact "smack in your face."[18] Lene perceives her gaze out of the frame as conveying *her own* masochistic pleasure to the off-screen viewer, not the sadist pirate wielding the whip. This dynamic would set up a rupture between the two instances of pleasure on either end of the whip: the pirates derive a collective homosocial pleasure from wielding the whip, a phallic surrogate, upon the female body that bolsters their patriarchal claim to women as property through erotic violence. Lene, conversely, finds ecstasy in the act of submission by retreating to the realm of fantasy, in this case one shared with the viewer and affirmed by the material riches she claims in the lyrics. If we follow the video's narrative, this argument holds little water. A curtain wipe in the middle of the chorus ups the ante on gendered violence with a shot of Lene struggling to keep her balance as her pirate captors goad her

---

18 Lyne Nyström, Interview with the author, October 13, 2022.

to walk the plank above a treacherous "sea" of billowing fabric waves and circling dorsal fins.

In typical camp fashion, ironic hyperbole accompanies jarring inversion with another rapid sawtooth wipe that, once again, cuts to a close-up of Lene. This time, however, she has inexplicably reversed her perilous position and wields a sword of her own (phalluses abound) and spars with all three pirates at once in a fast-motion scene. They cower and "Surrender!!" according to the subtitle. An iris shot transitions to Lene at the helm; she has shed her reflective pink for a rust-colored scoopneck dress that more closely matches the fiery red of her hair. She whips the crew into shape as they take bubble baths, shed tattered tunics for sumptuous overcoats, and consult a treasure map to chart a course for their destination. As the crew disembarks on a tropical island to claim their treasure, a grizzled old man (played by René) emerges from behind the foliage upon hearing the intruders. Subtitles and pantomime reveal that pirate-René is the old man's "silly son" and speed us through the video's denouement: the old man has had two daughters on the island—their otherness marked by faux-grass bikinis and caramel skin tone—who make convenient companions for Claus and Søren. Sitting around a fire, the old man whispers to Lene, "Actually, my son never had my sex appeal!" This revelation prompts Lene to coquettishly flirt with her captor-turned-crewman as the video closes with an iris cut onto their romantic embrace.

The two iris shots that come late in the video skew "My Oh My" away from the queer camp that permeates the interval between signifying lyrics and affective musicality in the song itself. This filmic technique often operates under the guise of humor—the Looney Tunes ocular opening is one famous example—and undergirds the narrative claims of cinema by formally anatomizing the camera as an eye; it goads the spectator into the scene by visually obviating the interpretation of a scene through the determination of a singular focal point. In the music video, the two uses of the iris shot follow the ambiguous scene of BDSM/violence and use the exaggeration of camp to entrench the track, as an audio-visual assemblage, in compulsory hetero-patriarchy even when women ostensibly reclaim a measure of independence. The first use of the technique arrives abruptly, moving outward from the center to rupture a narrative continuity and mark Lene's transition from captive to captain. This narrative shift *could* serve as a climactic fulcrum that inverts the power imbalance epitomized by sexual violence and legitimates Lene's leadership through the accumulation of capital (treasure). However, even this girl-boss feminist take falls flat as the video plays out and the technique is twined at the end of the video. The introduction of René as patriarch on a desert island reveals an endogamic machinery of gender to which Lene-as-princess was prisoner all along. There is something *too familiar* about the way René leans cheek-to-cheek with one daughter and winds his arm around the other. In the absence of a matriarch and totemic prohibition, this patriarch "gone native" may do more than entertain the taboo of incest.[19] Moreover, because René plays both father and "silly son"—a queer epithet if there ever was one—the Oedipal complex that would normally center on the objectified mother shifts to the desired princess Lene. These

---

[19]Sigmund Freud, "The Horror of Incest," in *Totem and Taboo* (London: Routledge Classics, 2001), 1–20.

visual signifiers ultimately unravel the campy belatedness scaffolded by the song to imbue her final conditional appeal—"If you were my king, I would be your queen"—with a desperate desire for subjugation not entirely dissimilar to Tiggy waiting alone on the other end of the line.

Above this formal reading of the song and video, there is still something to be said about the queerness fostered by camp's belatedness and the belated arrival of the video for "My Oh My." To what extent can the addition of a visual interpretation circumscribe the song's potential for multiple interpretive valences? Is the musical camp of "My Oh My" capable of shifting the video away from the choppy waters where a parodic evocation of kink sex slides into the violence endemic to patriarchy? The members of Aqua answer affirmatively, each in their own way, to say that the video's narratives are wholly distinct, secondary interpretations of, or supplemental to, the music itself.[20] But perhaps this belated video looms too large, eclipsing a queer reading between the lines of the song's forlorn feminine protagonist. The fraught queer camp elucidated through the sonic-symbolic recourse to a generalized pre-modern past in "My Oh My" represents only the first instance of Aqua's distinct capacity to perform a transgression that could pass as suitable for myriad audiences across geography, age, and culture. With their first global single, however, we find the plasticity of Aqua's tongue-and-cheek humor, prurient but not too vulgar, had its limits and was not immune to wildfire success and controversy.

---

[20] Dif, Interview with the author, November 11, 2022; Nyström, Interview with the author, October 13, 2022; Rasted, Interview with the author, October 10, 2022.

3 I'm a *Plastic* Girl

Aqua's "Barbie Girl" was inescapable during the summer and fall of 1997. Even in California's agricultural central valley, my childhood home, the song's almost too-giddy love for a fantastic life in plastic was a prominent feature of the pop radio I requested from the backseat; shiny background music in malls; and the prescribed introduction to coupling that was the school dance. I was cursorily aware of the "Barbie song," but only discovered Aqua at the birthday party of a classmate. Her family's ranch-style suburban home was perfectly pink; decked out in rose steamers, fuchsia balloons, hot pink tablecloths, and an ice cream cake piped in bubblegum foretelling the surprise treat within. I remember little of the festivities beyond one additional pink detail: a blush CD boombox given as a gift captivated the crowd of children as we danced around the living room cycling through tween hits. We all scatted along to Hansen's chorus, but it was Aqua's smash that garnered repeat requests across the already gendered boundaries of pop listening. Where I demurred into a practiced disinterest as they struck poses and debated who was which Spice Girl, "Barbie Girl" afforded me an opportunity to try on different genders without fear of ridicule. I could swing my hips a bit more and play at the fantasy of carefree girlhood embodied by Lene's exaggerated vocals so long as I also conveyed the playful obliviousness of René's oafish masculinity. While attributing a mythical trans origin story to "Barbie Girl" would give it far too much credit, the song's self-conscious kitsch in the age of Ellen DeGeneres and the ongoing HIV epidemic offers glimpses into gender's plasticity *because of*, not in spite of, its pop palatability on the world stage.

This chapter follows Aqua's meteoric rise to global stardom in 1997 by focusing on the marked plasticity of the discourse surrounding "Barbie Girl." Beginning our analysis one degree removed reveals a cohesive set of shared gender-essentialist assumptions about sexuality in late stage capitalist commodity culture that undergird aesthetic judgments, whether laudatory, disparaging, or ambivalent. The conflation of bad musical taste and misogynist objectification overtook the perception of a song that perplexingly defies circumscribed demographic spheres of pop listening. The song's reputation as kiddy-bop emblazoned with sexual inuendo is epitomized in the anglophone context by *Mattel, Inc. vs. MCA, Inc*, a highly publicized lawsuit filed by the maker of the doll almost immediately after the song's American release. However, this reception history only goes so far to explain Aqua's campy critique of a "life in plastic" and the endurance of "Barbie Girl" as a dance song emblematic of a bourgeoning millennial style with a distinctively queer afterlife. Loved and disdained, defended and ridiculed, a guilty pleasure or open secret, the camp that made "Barbie Girl" the defining song of Danish Bubblegum is ultimately the mechanism that fails to secure the gender critique it proffers. Yet, the plasticity of these aesthetic judgments (as *a priori* moral judgments) opens a space for a minor meaning-making when that camp is queer and specifically trans.[1] In this chapter, a trans-camp reading emerges from intersecting discursive valences that converge in formal qualities of "Barbie Girl" itself. The plastic of Barbie meets the plasticity associated with transness in this camp proposal, articulating itself between the lines of the between-the-lines as a formal investigation distinctive to the sensibility's recursive codes.

When Aqua returned to Denmark during the summer of 1997, after the Asian leg of their world tour, they were global stars. Lene recalls, "I think we only realized how successful the thing was after we'd come back from Asia, because while we'd been gone for so long all the papers had been writing about us."[2] And they often lauded Aqua. Writing for the Danish newspaper *Politiken*, Kim Skotte praised the originality of Aqua's frank and funny debut on the basis of their stage personae: "If the description 'dance-friendly pop music that nevertheless expresses something different in each song' doesn't sound like a shockingly original recipe, the infectious energy and unpretentious humor that radiates from Aqua is, on the other hand, palpable."[3] In a 1997 interview, René was shocked that Denmark's leading rock magazine gave *Aquarium* four stars

[1] Susan Stryker, *Transgender History: The Roots of Today's Revolution*, 2nd edn (Berkeley: Seal Press, 2009), 19. My definition of "trans" is rooted in the work of Susan Stryker who allows transgender to name "any and all kinds of variation from gender norms and expectations" and allows for a range of gender ontologies both within and beyond the Western circumscriptions of gender which transgender moves across (from the Latin root) to unravel the binary.
[2] Swift, *Aqua: The Official Book*, 33.
[3] Kim Skotte, "Pop der Holder Vand," *Politiken*, March 25, 1997. All translations from Danish are my own.

out of six when the group expected none.[4] But perhaps he shouldn't have been. The track also includes several riffs on the intersection of pop-rock and electronic music with surprising sophistication. When discussing the song's musical elements, Søren cited the guitar line in American House legend Todd Terry's remix of Everything But the Girl's "Missing" as a source of inspiration. Closer to home, the melody from acclaimed Danish pop-rap group Sound of Seduction's "Welcome to my World" inflected the display of Lene's own impressive range in the song's hook that also dramatically jumps across registers.[5]

The critical appraisal of Aqua was not unilaterally positive, however. An infamously scathing early review—one that the band still addresses only to point back to their success— in Denmark's popular newspaper *Ekstra Bladet* disparaged *Aquarium* with remarkable precision. Titled "Water in the Head," Morton V. Poulsen's subtitle predicted, "before the summer is over, thank god, the Danish-Norwegian Aqua will be buried in the deep well of oblivion." The one-star review was a mere two sentences: "You have to have spent quite a few hours in a dump of an aquarium while unconscious to think that this is cool. Both music and lyrics are so watered down and bubbly, devoid of substance, that Ace of Base seems like The Beatles in comparison."[6] Much like other international receptions of Aqua, the Danish rock critic did not deign to look for value

[4] René Dif, Claus Norreen, Lene Nystrøm, and Søren Rasted, Interview by Launch, *Launch*, 1997, Video, https://www.youtube.com/watch?v=O1DqXPU8Hcg..
[5] René Dif, Lene Nystrøm, and Søren Rasted, "Hvem er Aqua? 3:4," Interview by Søren Bygbjerg, *Hvem er?* DR Lyd, September 30, 2022, Audio, 60:01, https://www.dr.dk/lyd/p3/hvem-er/hvem-er-aqua-3-4.
[6] Morton V. Poulsen, "Vand i hovedet," *Ekstra Bladet*, April 17, 1997.

in a subgenre that was deemed even more worthless than the dance-pop of Sweden's biggest recent export. Poulsen was not alone in his vehement distaste for Aqua's popular success. Reinholdt Nielsen also couched his assessment of *Aquarium* in terms of rock musicality. "If the Barbie doll could sing, she would probably sound like the happy-pilled synthetic girl's voice, Lene Nysrøm, from the calculated hitlist success Aqua." He contends that *Aquarium* speculates on the market of the "youngest CD-consumers," implying their taste will be corrupted by Aqua's "aggravatingly monotonous drum programs" and "thoroughly bland collection of words delivered in a fresh up tempo." Nielsen, again like Poulsen, disparagingly compares Aqua to the progenitor of global Scandi-pop:

> Most of all, it sounds like a sped-up discount version of Abba topped with some irritating jingle-like bits of melody and the most flat and square drumbeat that you can edit on the computer yourself. The main point is that shit sells, and Aqua is a completely honest product, because it does not show off more than it can hold, and that, as has been said, isn't very much.[7]

Ouch!

The doubly damning accusation that *Aquairum* was devoid of substance in both music and lyrics follows the epistemological assumptions of rock criticism threatened by an impending shift in the taste for electronic pop music. For these Danish critics, placing Aqua among Swedish stars

---

[7] Reinholdt Nielsen, "Bare Barbie kunne synge," *Berlingske Tidende*, April 6, 1997.

Abba and Ace of Base judged their debut frivolous and mere consumerism, where other, less-qualified, vernacular critics might consider this an illustrious lineage of global pop success. As Simon Frith observed in 1998, conventional rock criticism "is driven by the need to differentiate: music is good because it is different, different from the run of 'mainstream' pop, different in the special intensity of feelings it brings about." These critics could not even be swayed by Aqua's live performances that eschew, as René put it in a 1997 interview, "the way of a normal pop band, with synchronic dancing. . . . Lene and me thought that it was much more fun to express a lot of energy and just freak out."[8] Aqua's desire to shift the tone of popular music with performance functioned similarly to Auslander's description of the glam performer who "questioned rock's ideology of authenticity by constructing overtly artificial personae" and revealing "the arbitrariness of performance personae" to parody even their own exaggerated style.[9] Nevertheless, Poulsen's and Nielsen's reviews are derisive, "so assessed by reference to a 'bad' system of production or to 'bad' social effect; cultural evaluation works by reference to social institutions or social behavior for which the music simply acts as a sign."[10] Aqua's effect in this instance is rather innocuous: *Aquarium*'s boring drum loops and vacuous lyrics are merely a product of the music industry, thereby lacking the "authenticity" of a proper performer and polluting the taste of music's youngest consumers.

[8] Dif, Norreen, Nyström and Rasted, Interview by Launch, 1997.
[9] Auslander, *Performing Glam Rock*, 185.
[10] Frith, *Performing Rites*, 69.

When "Barbie Girl" entered the American charts at a staggering number 7 on August 19, 1997, it seemed to appear out of nowhere; the result of strategic marketing maneuvers and radio inundation for the "year's infectious novelty number."[11] MCA devised a clever plan to organically break the single without a heavy marketing hand. They drew from the chance explosion of "The Look" by Swedish band Roxette in 1988 when an American student returned to Minnesota from a semester abroad with the CD and local airplay catapulted the group to fame in the states.[12] Although Aqua's publicity team could not force the serendipity of Roxette's success, they enlisted Copenhagen's CHR (contemporary hits radio) station to send copies of the single to American stations. In addition, they distributed white-label 12" records to DJs working in gay clubs outside of the country's largest urban queer populations, smaller markets with a taste for Eurodance, like San Antonio, Dallas, Miami, Orlando, Chicago, San Francisco, and Los Angeles.[13]

Alongside this initial success, when Aqua landed in the United States in September 1997, they found themselves embroiled in a highly publicized legal battle with the maker of Barbie. On September 11, Mattel sued MCA Records, Universal Denmark's parent company, in California's Central District Court based on the song's sexual subtext and sought an injunction

[11] Theda Sandiford-Waller, "Hot 100 Singles Spotlight," *Billboard*, August 19, 1997, 82.

[12] Jamie Feldman, "The Incredible True Story of How a College Student Launched Roxette To Fame In The U.S.," *Huffington Post*, December 12, 2019, https://www.huffpost.com/entry/dean-cushman-roxette_n_5df00aa5e4b0a59848d1e559.

[13] Anker, August 31, 2022; Theda Sandiford-Waller, "Hot 100 Singles Spotlight," *Billboard*, August 16, 1997, 82.

to halt distribution based on claims of copyright infringement, trademark dilution, and unfair competition. Mattel argued the song "misappropriated the Barbie trademark by using the word 'Barbie' in a way that would confuse consumers and damage the product line."[14] The damages Mattel claimed were in fact moral objections to the song's application of sexually adult themes to Barbie at odds with the doll's supposedly wholesome image. MCA responded with the assertion, "the Barbie doll has become an icon that means different things to different people," pointing out that the doll was already linked to her physical appearance, as both source of praise and criticism, and represented oppositional views concerning its relationship to feminism, chastity, and intelligence.[15] Applying these cultural observations to Aqua's song, MCA argued that "Barbie Girl" could not infringe Mattel's copyright because the song was a *parody*. Even Mattel found the parody argument difficult to sufficiently counter; in their rebuttal, they contradicted the foundational premise of infringement and dilution when they asserted that because the song was not about the doll, it could not be considered a parody.[16] In 1998, the Central District Court of California acknowledged that Barbie had acquired secondary meanings and judged in favor of the defendant on the grounds of parody, thus protecting the song as non-commercial speech under the first amendment. The judgment was upheld by the 9th Circuit Court of Appeals in 2002, and Judge William Matthew Byrne Jr. concluded his

---

[14] Mattel, Inc. v. MCA Records, Inc., No. CV 97-6791-WMIB, 1998 U.S. Dist. LEXIS 7310, at *6 (C.D. Cal. February 19, 1998).
[15] Ibid, at *11.
[16] *Mattel*, 28 F. Supp. 2d at 1125.

opinion with the infamous dismissal, "The parties are advised to chill."[17]

While the band shrugs off the lawsuit as overblown, with some subtext of a staged PR stunt, the exaggerated controversy ignited by *Mattel, Inc. vs. MCA, Inc.* established a discursive foundation for the band's American reception. Against Mattel's moral argument, MCA employed the legal language of parody to shift the accusation of moral indecorousness into the realm of ethics. In its legal sense, parody serves as a mechanism to defend against copyright infringement claims because, when designated a parody, the work in question is deemed to have exaggerated its imitation to the point that it serves as a criticism or commentary, most often signaled through humor, on its "original" source.[18] One of MCA's sticking points for their defense was the fact that Lene and René did not *resemble* Barbie and Ken in the video, but filtered the cultural symbols through their own stage personas. Importantly, this decision came from Lene herself. When she arrived on set Stenbæk presented her with a bleach blond wig so that she could fully embody the titular character. Lene summarily refused, insisting that she would not compromise her sartorial style to become conflated with a Barbie she was trying to critique, and delayed the video shoot while the directors called friends to find a couple who could play the part.[19]

Although the legal system twice ruled in favor of Aqua's hit on the basis of parody, the publicity surrounding the lawsuit

[17] Mattel, Inc. v. MCA Records, Inc. 296 F.3D (9th Cir. 2002), "Opinion," VI.
[18] Legal Information Institute, "Parody," Cornell University Law School, https://www.law.cornell.edu/wex/parody (accessed June 21, 2023).
[19] Nystrøm, October 13, 2022; *The Aqua Diary*, 1998.

permeated the American reception of "Barbie Girl." Whether a given critic judged the song positively or negatively, *Mattel, Inc. vs. MCA, Inc.* constructed a moral veil that determined its aesthetic value in advance: if "Barbie Girl" transforms the child's toy into a licentious sex-pot, then the song is bad on the heteronormative moral ground that it promotes superficial vanity and corrupts feminine chastity. Conversely, if "Barbie Girl," in fact, critiques these moral constraints and beauty standards imposed on women, the song is still bad because the lawsuit demonstrates its failure to successfully convey the terms of its parody.

The track occupies most of David Browne's attention in his album review for *Entertainment Weekly*, calling it "a dance-floor novelty that alludes to the secret, less-than-wholesome life of every little girl's favorite doll." He then evokes the lawsuit as a form of litigious justification for his conclusion that "bands like Aqua have a built-in obsolescence, particularly in these days of accelerated one-hit blunders." Browne does not even go so far as to consider the song a parody, but rather "a metaphor for the way women are sometimes manipulated by men—and sometimes manipulate themselves—for attention and success." The misogyny that lurks behind this critique should be clear; as a metaphor for women's malleability by men (and themselves?) "Barbie Girl" does not critique these conditions but merely plays into them. "Why bother suing?" asks Browne, "Even a Swedish meatball must realize that the song, with its rinky-dink, new-wave bounce, is the definition of disposable pop junk." Browne shifts from the lawsuit to the music to dismiss "the shamelessly derivative quality of their sound and songs." His only conciliatory praise of Aqua is given to René for "his Igor-in-heat croak insinuates its way into most of their songs. . . . He's the naughty drooler inside us all."[20] Browne's fantasy of masculine sexual access is articulated with the application of lecherous adjectives to René's timbre and shows the ambiguous registers of relation between persona and audience engendered by Aqua's hit. When analyzing the rhetoric of pop music criticism, Frith describes two uses of adjectives: "to relate the music to its possible uses . . . and to place it generically. In either case the purpose is consumer guidance. . . . Criticism, in other words, is not just producing a version of the music for the reader but also a version of the listener for the music."[21] In the case of "Barbie Girl," however, its insecure status as parody breaks down the ability for pop criticism to construct a listening public.

One the one hand, the disposability of dance-pop combined with the superficiality of a song about a toy would seem to securely align it with the bourgeoning tween market. As my own experience indicates, this was a song and video that resonated with the exploitation of children's fad consumerism bolstered by the band's colorful cartoon image. Other Eurodance bands took up this valence by recording club-ready songs that also functioned as toy advertisements. In 1998, Daze, one of Aqua's Danish contemporaries, released "Together Forever," their homage to the Tamagotchi, a handheld digital pet developed by the Japanese videogame company Bandai that swept the world in the late 1990s. Daze picks up a similar

[20] David Browne, "Album Review: Aquarium," *Entertainment Weekly*, October 17, 1997.
[21] Frith, *Performing Rites*, 68.

pseudo-Latin dance beat and hyper-saturated color scheme, but translates the mid-century plastic perfection of "Barbie Girl" into the virtual realm of video games. The following year, Spanish Eurodance group Blue4U took this trend to its natural extreme with "The Furby Song," a mind-numbing song that describes the furry robot's functions to a chorus that repeats the toy's name a whopping eleven times in four lines. Comparing these novelty songs to "Barbie Girl" reveals a crucial difference that stets "Barbie Girl" apart. The anthropomorphic toy speaks outside of the music in both Daze and Blue4U's tracks and mimics the form of engagement one would have with each toy. Distinct from these two songs that are more securely geared toward young listeners, the internal dialogic structure established from the start of "Barbie Girl" embeds the lyrics within a musical landscape that sets the object apart from the world in which it intervenes, reinforced by René and Lene's retention of their own personae in the video.

On the other, the erotic implications of its lyrics, misinterpreted literally, conjoined to a club beat perplexingly lead the critic back toward an adult audience that should judge the song comically bad based on its inanity. This productive misinterpretation is reflected in the lewd parodies that sprang up in the wake of "Barbie Girl." Only a month after Aqua hit the American stage, journalist Theda Sandiford-Waller reported two parodies making their way across the radio waves:

> WHTZ New York is airing the parody "Bimbo Girl" by Dave Kolin. Radio syndicator United Stations Radio Networks says that 70 stations are airing Kolin's parody. Here's a taste of the lyrics: "I'm a bimbo girl in a bimbo world/My boobs are plastic, isn't that

fantastic?" Eddie V of WBBM Chicago's morning show created his answer to "Barbie Girl" called "Ken Doll," which goes in part: "I'm a Ken doll. I'm no fun at all/You know I'll fail ya, I got no genitalia."[22]

Another interpretation also called "Bimbo Girl" came from the UK radio host Chris Moyles. Moyles's version drops all pretense and plays Barbie as a brainless tart who describes herself as "dim, thick, and easy." Ken is a chauvinist slag who opens with "come on silly, touch my . . ." (interrupted before we get the phallic rhyme), praises only her looks with "fake breasts [that] will explode," and demeans Barbie's intelligence. Obsessing over what's on Barbie's chest and not between Ken's legs reveals more than a regression into inquisitive childhood fantasies. These gauche spoofs predicated on the misrecognition of "Barbie Girl" as not-parody attempt to constrain the song to an endorsement of consumerist materialism imposed upon the commodified sexualization of the bimbo as a woman rendered object through the surface of her body and the expense of any interiority. These ethical judgments that cry misogyny and objectification are the result of a double failure: the anglophone (American) public's failure to recognize "Barbie Girl" as parody, and the song's failure to convey its status as parody because it confounded the capacity to discursively construct an audience.

To this point, the critical discourse around "Barbie Girl" demonstrates a remarkable multiplicity of interpretations that

---

[22]Theda Sandiford-Waller, "Hot 100 Singles Spotlight," *Billboard*, September 27, 1997, 115.

all depend on the song's legibility as parody and ultimately produce a glorification of the bimbo as a slut eager to submit to the objectifying patriarchal gaze. It is precisely the plasticity of Aqua's fantastic life in plastic (i.e., global late stage capitalism) that also signals the possibility to assess the parodic content of Aqua's hit as one facet of its camp, as my emphasis on legal parody anticipates. Sontag recognizes parody as a critical quality of camp in her seminal characterization of the sensibility. When distinguishing high (or pure, naïve) camp from low (or deliberate) camp, Sontag opines, "Probably intending to be campy is always harmful" as a result of "the delicate relationship between parody and self-parody in Camp." For Sontag, camp is about a purity of extremes. If the self-parodic element is tainted by a "contempt for one's themes, one's materials . . . the results are heavy handed, rarely Camp. . . . Camp is either completely naïve," that is to say unaware of its own traffic in camp, "or else wholly conscious (when one plays at being campy)."[23]

Of course, certain critics were in on the joke and praised camp elements of "Barbie Girl" without naming them as such. Larry Flick wrote:

Leave it to a European act to cook up such a deliciously over-the-top send-up of America's most beloved doll. With her squeaky, high-pitched delivery, Lene Grawford Nystrom fronts this giddy pop/dance diddy as if she were Barbie, gleefully verbalizing many of the twisted things people secretly do with the doll. At the same time, she effectively rants about the inherent misogyny of Barbie with a subversive hand. Rene Dif

[23] Sontag, "Notes on Camp," 282–3.

is an equally playful and biting presence, as he embodies male counterpart Ken with an amusing leer.[24]

In fact, "Barbie Girl" was single of the week with a shining five stars in *Music Week* on October 4, 1997, and recognized for its cleverness: "Bleached and blond this bouncy Euro pop tune may be, but dumb it isn't. Its mix of perky vocals, barbed lyrics and infectious energy has already brought it success in Scandinavia and the U.S."[25] Integral qualities of camp emerge as the fulcrum around which the song's positive attributes revolve. The critics hinge their assessment on the capacity to recognize and derive pleasure from the humorous critique that emerges between the lines of the lyrics and the subtext imbued to them by the musical performance.

Inadvertently, these critics' assessments align with 1990s queer reevaluations of camp that rely heavily on Linda Hutcheon's postmodern theory of parody. Parody is a form of "ironic inversion . . . playing with multiple conventions," a "trans-contextualization" structured by "extended repetition with critical difference." For Hutcheon, it bestows the reader (or decoder) with an interpretive agency independent of the author because parody requires "the decoder construct a second meaning through inference about surface statements and supplement the foreground with acknowledgement and knowledge of a background context."[26] In Moe Meyer's polemical reclamation, the critical recursivity of parody

[24]Larry Flick, "New and Noteworthy," *Billboard*, August 16, 1997, 62.
[25]Simon Abbott et al., "Single of the Week," *Music Week*, October 4, 1997, 30.
[26]Linda Hutcheon, *The Theory of Parody: The Teachings of Twentieth-Century Art Forms* (New York: Methuen, 1985), 6–7, 34–5.

reinvests camp with politics when it "emerges as specifically queer parody possessing cultural and ideological analytic potential, taking on new meanings with implications for the emergence of a theory that can provide an oppositional queer critique."[27] He situates parodic creation in the (queer) readers who reshape objects that were not intended for them and enter "alternative signifying codes into discourse by attaching them to existing structures of signification." Camp has the enormous task of being "the only process by which the queer is able to enter representation and to produce social visibility."[28]

Meyer's claim to social radicality as the sole means of queer visibility comes at the expense of what might be camp's greatest strength, the contingencies and contradictions of a reading practice determined by an aesthetic code that not all spectators can decipher. Chuck Kleinhans shifts the terms of Meyer's insistence on identitarian political exceptionalism. He points to the pitfalls that emerge when parody's discursive role "rests on the assumption that parody creates an 'open form' that allows for a complex experience. The text then becomes open (or free), producing a liberating effect on the audience (though we might remember that freedom can only be taken, not given)."[29] This open form can as easily be liberatory and employed as a "means of control and domination." Yet parody as an integral component of camp can and has, more innocuously but no less harmfully, been taken up by the culture industry in the form of what Kleinhans calls "het camp," or the

---

[27] Meyer, "Introduction," *The Politics and Poetics of Camp*, ed. Moe Meyer, 10.
[28] Ibid., 11.
[29] Chuck Kleinhans, "Taking out the Trash: Camp and the Politics of Parody," in *The Politics and Poetics of Camp,* ed. Moe Meyer, 197.

dilution of camp's critical edge following Sontag's erasure of queerness as the non-hegemonic interpretive condition at its foundation. Kleinhans's conclusion is ultimately on the side of camp, "as parody, has an ability to expose what the powers-that-be would like to keep neatly hidden and out of sight. . . . Camp can insist on a determined recycling of political agendas as well as aesthetic diversity."[30]

But what if the camp object fails itself? What if "self-aware kitsch" asserts its parodic commentary on hegemonic norms only in terms acceptable to the neoliberal feint of critique as assimilable progress that maintains the status quo? Are there other forms that might reside outside the binary of liberatory visibility (as agential discoursing) and the deceptive banality of het camp? Is there a camp reading that depends on a parodic critique of the critique? In other words, might the shortcomings of "Barbie Girl"'s commentary on heteronormative femininity be reflexively read back onto the song itself? Can the song's failure to make its critique adequately legible in fact gesture toward queerer spaces of camp that eschew overt visibility and locate an ephemeral expressivity in the ironic parody of hypersexual bimboization, another reading practice that emerges from forms that fail their own self-awareness? The answer may be yes, from a trans-feminist lens, if we consider the queer club an essential factor in "Barbie Girl"'s success.

And the club appeal of "Barbie Girl"'s remixes proved to be a fruitful ground from which to locate Aqua's queerly diverse audiences. Notably, the single release that included club remixes garnered a unique commentary on the song. James

---

[30] Ibid., 199.

Hyman's review begins by generically identifying "Barbie Girl" as a "Balearic-tinged Euro pop smash hit."[31] Balearic first emerged in Ibiza in the late 1980s as a DJ-ing approach that eschewed stylistic fidelity and codes of taste for an eclectic mix of dance and non-dance songs and in the 1990s developed into genre fusing deep house with laid-back, swing-beat elements of R&B, Latin, African, and funk.[32] To locate a "tinge" of the genre in Aqua points to the sense of carefree summer fun that propels the track with four-four bass kicks, light hi-hats that hit between beats, and the light swing of conga rolls from one measure to the next. Where most critics considered "Barbie Girl" only within a narrow conception of Scandi-pop, Hyman sees the forest for the trees to position Aqua as a crossover from Eurodance by isolating trends in the remixes of "Barbie Girl." He compares the track to the 1994 trans-Atlantic hit "Another Night" by Real McCoy—a German Eurobeat group who also had a paired female vocalist and male rapper. The "Perky Park Club Mix" is "ultra-flavoured, organ prodding, synth rising," and "Spike's Anatomically Correct Dub" is described as "a quarter of the way to Van Helden," the American House remixer par excellence, because of its "digi-vocoding and looped phrases like René's 'Wanna go for a ride?'"

The sonic club meets the visual school yard in a concluding observation: "My niece refuses to go to bed unless the video is played several times over; I think that speaks for itself with

[31] James Hyman, "Hot Vinyl: Tune of the Week," *Music Week,* September 13, 1997.
[32] For more on Balearic see: Bill Bruster and Frank Broughton, *Last Night a DJ Saved My Life: The History of the Disc Jockey* (New York: Grove Press, 2006); Simon Reynolds, *Energy Flash: A Journey Through Rave Music and Culture* (Berkeley: Soft Skull Press, 2012).

regard to ongoing single success."[33] Although Hyman delivers this line as obvious, it is telling insofar as it departs from a singular construction of *the listener*, identified in Frith's analysis of pop criticism, favoring the unexpected coexistence of ravers (on the beach or in the nightclub) and adolescents (specifically young girls). Importantly, he does so without replicating the dichotomy this chapter has traced thus far. Rather than rely on the (il)legibility of "Barbie Girl"'s lyrics as parody to justify aesthetic critique in ethical claims, Hyman's five-star evaluation assesses Lene's "squeaks" and René's "frisky retorts" with the same scrutiny as the musical composition of the remixes and, cursorily, the video.

Sample-based electronic musician Carl Stone similarly privileges "Barbie Girl"'s formal elements over signifying meaning in his dismantled and reconfigured composition "Flint's" from the 2007 album *Al-Noor*.[34] The track follows Stone's sampling technique that resembles its source material "at some point in the course of the piece but at another point I would dare say it sounds very different. . . . It's taking something that's familiar and making it unfamiliar." "Flint's"'s resemblance is uncanny: its opening lumbers, a lone organ melody line you just cannot quite place punctuated by heavy kick-drum beats. Pitched-down vocals run backward and unravel a linear progression. With two sharp down beats on a snare, the tempo suddenly jolts, dropping certain elements to catch up as the pitch rises. Now the voice achieves Lene's timbre

---

[33] Hyman, "Hot Vinyl: Tune of the Week."
[34] My thanks to Thomas Love who brought this track to my attention early in my research.

augmented by a squeal reminiscent of a tape rewinding. It is joined by René's gruff voice reduced to minimal clips of words. In "Flint's," these distorted vocals present what Jarman-Ivens theorizes as a queer "ontology of the voice" defined by "its capacity always-already to detach the signifier of the vocal wave form from the signified of the identity of the voice's producer." These uncannily familiar phrasings produce a kind of déjà vu in Stone's track and "keep open the possibility for multiple gender identities, at least until such time as identity is conferred upon the voice's producer by the listener."[35] And this is precisely the process Stone employs when he cleverly reveals his source material about two-thirds of the way into the nine-and-a-half-minute track when Lene's palindromic "ooh-oh-ooh" that signals the start of the chorus cannot hide from Stone's disorienting not-quite-remix.

Stone began experimenting with Aqua's hit at least seven years before releasing "Flint's." In a 2000 interview, Stone and Aqua unexpectedly collide during a discussion about the belatedness of intellectual property in the digital age, a topic at the heart of Stone's musical practice. When the interviewer pointed to the topical lawsuit surrounding "Barbie Girl," Stone disclosed his "horrified fascination with that song as material for some live performances."[36] Stone's sample of "Barbie Girl" is often evoked to characterize his taste, which one interviewer says indicates that there "doesn't seem to be any distinction between high or low, or any snobbery to it, there's nothing

[35] Jarman-Ivens, *Queer Voices*, 3.
[36] Frank J. Oteri, "Carl Stone: Intellectual Property, Artistic License and Free Access to Information in the Age of Sample-Based Music and the Internet," American Music Center, October 17, 2000.

winking about it."[37] "Nothing winking," another way to say nothing camp, or, according to a different interviewer, "a thrill" in the "deconstruction" of "trashy pop music" into something more worthwhile. But Stone's compositional complexity and innovative sampling do not shy away from the coded wink. Rather, the sophistication of "Flint's" stages a disorienting encounter that defamiliarizes "Barbie Girl" through a formal engagement with camp. An inference Stone nuances when he places "Barbie Girl" in his "two-dimensional matrix" of music categorization as "music I love but don't respect."[38] Is loving without (earnestly) respecting the object not the epitome of camp's eccentric reading method?

Like Stone, the cover by the duo Gendered Dekonstruktion (comprised of Toronto-based DJ and producer Callum Magnum and an anonymous collaborator) uses formal elements of the original to deconstruct, as their name suggests, and reconfigure "Barbie Girl" with the loving irreverence of non-binary queer camp. Gendered Dekonstruktion retains the tonic of C# to musically emphasize the continuity with the original track but transforms the summer jam into hypnotic peak hours techno and psytrance. The bass drum becomes an open thud; sixteenth notes tick on a hi-hat; the hard trace bassline is crunchy and distorted; and a laser fires in quadruplets atop. Characteristic of Gendered Dekonstruktion tracks, the cover

---

[37] Emily Bick, "A Two-Dimensional Matrix: Carl Stone Speaks to Emily Bick," *The Wire*, March 2019, https://www.thewire.co.uk/in-writing/interviews/carl-stone-interview-by-emily-bick.

[38] Ibid.; Todd L. Burns, "Charting Carl Stone's Musical Evolution: Sampling the Sacred and Profane," *Red Bull Music Academy*, December 5, 2016, https://daily.redbullmusicacademy.com/2016/12/carl-stone-interview/.

employs a text-to-speech voice that monotonously repeats a single phrase until the signifying content dissolves into the enthralling composition. In this case, various iterations of "I can beg on my knees" tuned to C#4 repeats, occasionally interrupted by declamations of "Barbie Girl" tuned one octave lower. The extracted lyric is a flirtatious sexual invitation that opens onto myriad pleas in Gendered Dekonstruktion's deracinated sonic landscape. The composition's hypnotic thrall combined with the agendered voice produces a cyborgian meld human and machine.[39] Feminist theorist Donna Haraway laid the foundation for a feminism where "the cyborg is a kind of disassembled and reassembled postmodern collective and personal self."[40] The cyborg has been taken up by other trans, ecocritical, and decolonial scholars to engage and critique the post-, trans-, and inhuman as a liberatory future outside of an oppressive present.[41] While this sentiment is shared by Gendered Dekonstruktion, the agendered potential of the digital voice becomes a site of ephemeral envelopment on the dancefloor rather than a promised future.[42] The cover offers a form of parody as "a paradoxical structure of contrasting

---

[39] Callum Magnum, email to the author, August 9, 2023.

[40] Donna Haraway, *Simians, Cyborgs, and Women: The Reinvention of Nature* (New York: Routledge, 1991), 163.

[41] Stacy Alaimo, *Bodily Nature: Science, Environment, and the Material Self* (Bloomington: University of Indiana Press, 2010); Jasbir Puar, "I'd Rather Be A Cyborg Than a Goddess: Becoming Intersectional in Assemblage Theory," *Philosophia* 2, no. 1 (2012): 49–66; Jeanne Vaccaro, "Feeling Fractals: Wooly Ecologies of Transgender Matter," *GLQ: A Journal of Lesbian and Gay Studies* 21, no. 2–3 (2015): 273–93.

[42] Provenzano, "Making Voices," 81–2. My assertion of the liberatory potential of the cyborgian digital voice affirms Provenzano's suggestion of possibilities that might emerge in "the broken or uncertain boundary between human and machine" as they relate to queer genders.

synthesis, a kind of differential dependence of one text upon another."[43] The camp in this instance does not depend on a humorous critique. Rather, highlighting one of the song's most suggestive lyrics allows for queer pleasure and urgent plea to coexist.

Hyman's dance-centered review, Stone's defamiliarized sampling technique, and Gendered Dekonstruktion's cyborgian cover offer interrelated formal approaches to see and hear trans-camp relations in Aqua's ubiquitous hit. However, to listen for a trans dimension of queer camp might seem to move perilously close to undermining transgender embodiment as mere gender parody. Valorizing a trans-camp sensibility, therefore, could appear regressive in the ongoing struggle for transgender dignity and protection against the violence faced by trans (and disproportionately trans-of-color) individuals. With its visibility in the wake of queer theory, transness has been made to bear queer radicality by embodying gender's mutable plasticity, thereby undermining the power of Western hetero-patriarchy predicated upon the disenfranchisement of queers and people of color through binarized gender.[44] As Marissa Brostoff elucidates, this facet of queer camp threatens to demean "a politics of trans sincerity, in which the gender-nonconforming subject is celebrated as transgressive to the extent that her nonconformity can be read as *serious*—that is, to the extent that she rejects camp. . . . Authenticity has once again become the byword of liberatory gender politics but

---

[43] Hutcheon, *The Theory of Parody*, 61.
[44] Kadji Amin, "Trans* Plasticity and the Ontology of Race and Species," *Social Text* 143 (2020): 49–71.

is attached, this time around, to the transgender body itself." Brostoff argues that this shift to a normative legitimation of trans embodiment based on its seriousness and authenticity holds parallels with the recent swapping of culture for sex practice as the criterion for participation in gay male life. "Yet, this state of affairs—which, in the case of both transgender (particularly trans-feminine) and gay male aesthetics, pivots on camp— exists in tension with one that has been more often remarked upon: the self-conscious absorption of camp aesthetics into a wide swath of mainstream media productions."[45] Weaving between its disavowal and mainstream cooptation, camp nevertheless remains a productive reading practice because it can function in a mode akin to Muñoz's disidentification, defined in the introduction as the performed reading of a cultural field by a minoritarian subject without recourse to hegemonic authority.[46] A trans-centered queer camp reads beyond authenticity and seriousness, between its parodic relation to mainstream media, and as a formal quality that fails to fully adhere to its objects.

The plasticity of "Barbie Girl" as parody traced in a variety of forms throughout this chapter opens onto a potential trans-camp interpretation precisely because of the malleable coherence of its ironic reading practice that holds in tension the seemingly antithetical registers of earnestness and humor, blind consumerist misogyny and its critique, all rooted in the visions of femininity that emerge between listener and song.

---

[45] Brostoff, "Notes on Caitlyn, or Genre Trouble: On the Continued Usefulness of Camp as Queer Method," 1–18.
[46] Muñoz, *Disidentifications*, 15, 25.

Moreover, the plasticity of a trans-camp attentive to "the power relations, conceptual genealogies, and biopolitical economies brought into play when putatively distinct orders of being are materially combined" refuses to delimit its liberatory potential.[47] Trans-camp understands that its small discursive act might be coopted back into the neoliberal matrix of gender economies, whether with resignation or resentment. It thereby aligns itself with the pleasure of camp's mutability where even oppositional meaning-making can be camped with the cultural objects and interpretations that might oppress us.

Trans-camp's doubled doublespeak traced throughout this chapter coalesces in the second cover of "Barbie Girl" from Evelyn and Scotia, two trans-women musicians and DJs based in New York. The new-wave synth bass line that oscillates across an octave on pairs of eighth notes and the stripped-down lento kick drum and snare percussion camps Aqua's ironic peppiness by reversing the tone into goth's feigned unapproachability. René's raspy greeting, "Hi Barbie," is pitched down to a slow-motion frog croak, wearing its post-production modification on its sleeve. In Scotia's hands, the ingenuous naïveté of Lene's timbre metamorphoses into a Lolita's premature worldly nonchalance. Combined with the relaxed tempo and ethereal tremolo synths, Scotia's teasingly sexy half-sung alto delivery sounds like a girl who's too good for the Valley so she parties in Los Angeles. The synthetic quality of this cover looks to the macabre side of a life in plastic to bring sex to the fore. This is almost diametrically opposed to other

---

47 Amin, "Trans* Plasticity," 66.

contemporary dance riffs on Aqua's hit like Aiden Francis's proggy bop "Plastic Fantasy" and the Australian-Canadian duo DJ Chrysalis and Regularfantasy who rerecorded vocals that repeat "life in plastic, it's fantastic." In this cover, Scotia embodies the bimbo's performative vacuousness with such flair that she might affirm the ribald eroticism of the parodies that sprung up in "Barbie Girl"'s wake.

However, Scotia's vocals and Evelyn's instrumentation employ a trans camp that ensures sleaze does not equate to misogynist exploitation. Near the song's midpoint, the breathy delivery of the chorus begins to echo at different pitches creating a reverberating harmony that is all Scotia's voice. When the absurdly deep pitch of Ken's part reenters, the fact that all these voices are Scotia's dawns on the listener. The duo has cleverly used the trans-feminine voice to play on the gendered dichotomy of the original. These manipulated vocals achieve the fullness of camp by ironically playing with the trans queerness of Scotia's voice as gendered a posteriori, as already discussed via Jarman-Ivens. By singing across the masculine and feminine divide—as we will also see with The Moon Baby in the next chapter—Scotia ironically embodies both the sexualized bimbo and her throaty suitor. Rather than shy away from Barbie's vapidity, Scotia and Evelyn lean into plasticity, drawing out the sexual agency that can be claimed from the bimbo's objectification. They relish the hyperfeminine sexuality that Aqua wrote as a critique and embrace the fact that Aqua's parody failed to clearly convey its support for a woman's agency beyond her appearance. Bolstered by shifting the song's cheery daytime disposition into the depths of the night, they turn it on its head to articulate a trans-camp engagement with the global hit. They do not endorse the reduction of women's sexuality to that of a passive object, nor do they deny its power. The cover leans into the parodic excess of Aqua's bimbo Barbie whose fame is acquired with her body, as if to say: "My beauty may be manipulated, my stupidity may be feigned, my sexuality may be wanton, but my womanhood is unimpeachable."

4 I'm an *Exotic(izing)* Girl

Hot on the heels of "Barbie Girl"'s infectious global take-over, Aqua continued to prove their staying power and international appeal. In an appearance on Britain's Top of the Pops in October 1997 "Barbie Girl" was still at number 1, beating out Natalie Imbruglia's "Torn" and "Tell Him," the duet by divas Barbara Streisand and Céline Dion. Following their British appearance, the band performed in Paris, where *Aquarium* had achieved gold, and Rotterdam for a crowd of 18,000 fans who knew every word.

Now that Aqua had become a household name across the globe and in the midst of this demanding touring schedule, Aqua returned to Denmark in the early fall of 1997 to ensure their continued success and film back-to-back videos for the fourth and fifth singles from *Aquarium*—"Doctor Jones" and "Lollipop (Candyman)." "Doctor Jones" was positioned as a follow-up to "Barbie Girl" that would dispel assumptions that they were a novelty band or a one-hit wonder. The single was released in October 1997 with an Australian release in December and in the UK in January of the following year. Although "Doctor Jones" hit the top of the charts throughout Europe and the commonwealth markets of Australia, New Zealand, and Canada, it failed to make a splash in Japan and the United States—with the exception of the American Club charts. In many ways the two singles form an interesting pair with their tonal relation (in C-minor and C#-minor, respectively), the successful formula of a call-and-response love song between high "feminine" and low "masculine" vocals, and the use of kitschy cinematic tropes in both videos. Yet, this chapter begins from the assertion that the two singles stand as exemplars of Aqua's camp not for their sameness, but because they diverge at several crucial junctures while using a nearly identical repertoire of musical and visual techniques. "Barbie Girl" translates a grooving summer beat into a confectionary treat for the masses by presenting a music video that blended the club-ready composition itself with an erotic camp parody staged between iconic childhood toys. "Doctor Jones" is similarly rooted in the house and Balearic tracks produced to keep Europeans partying long after their summer holiday; think of the smash hit "Bailando" by the Belgian outfit Paradiso that swept the continent in 1996 but achieved its greatest success in Scandinavia. "Doctor Jones"'s popularity on the dance charts and the sophisticated reinterpretations offered by the single's remixes are indicative of its difference from "Barbie Girl." But the contrast between these two singles is most evident in the relationship between their audio and visual elements as conveyers of camp significatory possibilities. "Barbie Girl" coheres around a singularity between song and video, to the point that one is nearly inseparable from the other. By contrast there are two distinct strains of camp operating in "Doctor Jones" that rest on the difference between the song—which is fundamentally a club track that seeks broad appeal through the translation of a jejune and purposefully vague narrative of love—and the video that translates it into a spectacle of colonial hijinks in the primitive tropics. Together these discrepant forms of camp produce a fraught discordance between the multiple meanings offered by the song and the singularity of the video's brand of neo-colonial exoticism.

With a chorus of chirping cicadas and the soft hoot of birds, "Doctor Jones" sets a mood of evening warmth as a sustained organ chord rises in the mix alongside the pluck of a guitar melody that establishes the chord structure. Lene's voice enters with the sighing satisfaction of new love, "Sometimes, the feeling is right/you fall in love for the first time" before turning to the corporeal sensations of heartbeats and sweet kisses that are associated with "summertime love in the moonlight." Lene yodels her joy in a series of "ah-yippi-ah-yi-ooh"'s as the introduction of a kick drum builds suspense before a sweeping whoosh sends the song into the stars. In the first verse, we learn that this summer romance has ended and Lene's remembrance is tinged with the melancholy of loneliness. The track effectively stages a simulated exchange between the distanced lovers as they alternate pronouncements of longing, continued interest, and hyperbolic romance in the pre-chorus: "You swept my feet/right off the ground/you're the love I found."

As the first verse and pre-chorus make clear, "Doctor Jones" depends on its ability to camp the clichéd tropes of heterosexual romance by narrating them at a physical distance and playing up sentimentality's vacuity by eliding lyrical specificity in favor of emotional vocal timbre. In the song's three minutes and twenty-four seconds, there are only the vaguest indications of a narrative past. "Doctor Jones" plays itself out in the ephemeral moment of communication—whether epistolary, by telephone, or email, we have no idea—of a love that cannot be affirmed physically and is thus without assurance and must be held on to. The lyrical evocation of the affective intensity, immediacy, instantaneity of infatuation lends itself to the track's orientation as ready for the summer love(s) found in chance encounters on the dancefloor.

Another halcyon breeze blows the chorus in. The song takes a perplexing turn as Lene names her suitor in the third person, repeating the titular "Doctor Jones, Jones/Calling Doctor Jones," imploring him to wake up. René echoes the call to "wake up now," a peculiar interjection given the fact he is the presumed object of Lene's command. However, there is scant lyrical indication that Doctor Jones is the lover who left his partner at the end of the summer. In fact, the second verse stages the possibility of two simultaneous conversations: the first pair of lines reveals an obsessive melancholy where all Lene can think of is her lover, addressed as "you," while the second pair seems to be directed at Jones as she implores, "Doctor, what can I do?/Why does it have to be like that?" The bridge heightens the ambiguity as Lene begs, "Please, please, cure me" fourfold to no one in particular. We lose the love story entirely in the breakdown and repetition of the chorus as a denouement where the proper name "Jones" is repeated eighteen times in the final fifty seconds (amounting to about a quarter of the song).

Perhaps the irresolution of this prattling exchange between a forlorn lover and her physician (who may also be her lover) is precisely the point. When describing his process for writing the lyrics to "Doctor Jones," Søren cited an unexpected reference, the Counting Crows' 1993 "Mr. Jones." Claus and Søren pulled from a wide breadth of pop musical sources when composing *Aquarium*. Yet, this inspiration from an alternative rock hit functions slightly differently than "Barbie Girl"'s riffs on Everything But the Girl and Sound of Seduction. The combination of meaningless refrains and the repetition of the common last name "Jones" in the Counting Crows' song offered an example of the extent to which the simultaneous specificity and generality of a proper noun can effectively drive a song without hemming in a narrative too tightly. While writing the song with Claus and Anders Øland, Søren remembers shifting Mr. Jones to Doctor Jones because the repetition was catchy. It was never meant to make it into the final version: "They were repeating Jones quite a lot . . . we thought that was cool . . . but I always thought, 'Well, we're going to change it soon. . . .' But nobody ever asked me . . . so we never changed it."[1] The fact that the titular "Jones" was a placeholder that could be replaced with any other surname indicates that from its inception "Doctor Jones" was not intended to elicit its primary connection to the listener by way of a defined narrative. Rather the song traffics in Eurodance songwriting, where lyrics often eschew narrative coherence to augment the song's musicality. In other words, "Doctor Jones" is much more akin to "Roses are Red" insofar as its primary goal is not to tell a story in song, but to get bodies moving.

And it would seem that Aqua was, yet again, successful. When "Doctor Jones" was reviewed in the pan-European industry publication *Music & Media*, comparisons to other

---

[1] Rasted, October 10, 2022.

hits from *Aquarium* were at hand: "The motto 'if it ain't broke don't fix it' seems to have been the creed of the Aqua team when they came up with this worthy successor to the phenomenon that iss [*sic*] *Barbie Girl*." Yet, this review did not dismiss the follow-up single as derivative. "Not only is it a strong pop song in its own right, but the inclusion of some tasty remixes by Antiloop and Molella & Phil Jay among others could arouse interest from programmers who usually chart their course away from the mainstream."[2] This focus on the remixes as evidence for the strength of the original is crucial to recognizing the distinct contribution of "Doctor Jones" to *Aquarium*'s success as a song first and video second, where the majority of Aqua's singles functioned as a confluence of music and moving image. The European reviewer astutely singles out the two most innovative. Antiloop was a Swedish trance and house duo formed in 1994 by David Westerlund and Robin Söderman. When they produced their remix, they had recently released their debut LP and been named the best house/techno act by the Swedish Dance Music Awards. Their interpretation of "Doctor Jones" transforms the bubbly summer dance track into a hard trance extravaganza built for the club. Like the original, the "Antiloop Club Mix" opens by creating an atmosphere, but here it is the muffled thud of a pounding subwoofer, signaling the periphery of the club. The springy pulsing bass pulled from the hard bounce subgenre drives the track, with the addition of sixteenth-note snares to build suspense, and a sharp, flanged melody line that soars across the track with typical trance melodrama. Antiloop

---

[2]"Airborne," *Music & Media* 15, no. 1–3 (January 17, 1998), 16.

removes any notion of a narrative of forlorn love and homes in on a similar strategy to Søren's inclination to use "Jones" for its sonic quality rather than signifying content. René's verses are excised from the ten-minute track, and the majority the song loops a small snippet of Lene's "ah-yippi-ah-yi-ooh" that shifts to her repetition of "Doctor Jones" only to punctuate the drops. Antiloop's transformation of Aqua's fourth single into a dynamic trance anthem which values foreshadowed, atmospheric repetition over jarring musical shifts in mood—accentuates the original's emphasis on danceability over narrative. Perhaps this is why the "Antiloop (Club) Mix" remains one of Aqua's most listened-to remixes.[3]

The second remix mentioned in the review, by Italo-house duo Molella and Phil Jay (Maurizio Molella and Filippo Carmeni), offers another angle into "Doctor Jones." Cicadas and birds are transformed into a synth patch that sounds like something between a hooting owl and the drip of water. An overdrive guitar oscillates across an octave as the kick drums on the beat and a high-hat hisses on the offbeat. It would seem that Lene's yodeling is the most captivating facet of the song because the duo also makes it the thematic centerpiece of their remix, clipping "ah" to a quadruplet and allowing the phrase to float mellifluously over the distilled house elements. Distinct from the late night mood of Antiloop's hard trace interpretation, Molella and Phily Jay retain the song's pop verse-chorus structure, and strip down the original's lighthearted summery sentiments to a swaying house vibe ready for a day party. This cover typifies the marketing strategy for Aqua's remixes

---

[3] Anker, August 31, 2022.

with its groovy bassline and isolation of a single vocal hook to provide continuity from the club to radio. Often these remixes were initially targeted to southern European markets so that they might be played in clubs frequented by locals and tourists alike, who would then take the earworm wherever they called home.[4] When speaking to *Music & Media*, Stefano Carboni, an Italian music director for a radio station in Milan, suggested "that *Doctor Jones* has a perfect prescription for a pop/dance crossover hit. 'I think it's very much in line with what is happening over here,' elaborating, 'It is a very clever commercial project, and they are reaching a massive audience in both the pop and the dance areas this way.'"[5]

In their cover of the track, The Moon Baby (Barbara Bliss, a Philadelphia-based musician and drag performer) and J-Cow (Josh Cowgill, a Berlin-based producer and DJ) return this commercial project to the club and employ the trans voice to camp Aqua's heterosexual love story. The track holds to its referent with an ambient layer of insect chirps, but J-Cow replaces the arpeggiated synth-guitar melody with a patch that mimics the breathy expansiveness of a pan flute. It moves on doublets down a fourth, up a third, and up another third before returning to the tonic. Where Aqua's version maintains the energy with a bass line of staccato triplets, a pounding four-four kick, and sweeping ornamentation in the upper register, J-Cow transports "Doctor Jones" from peak hours to the swaying dancefloor of a warm summer daybreak. The cover is rhythmically driven with an alternating kick and hi-hat

[4] Ibid.
[5] "Airborne," 16.

accompanied by a snare breakbeat as the melody floats above with plenty of reverb for color (think of Cisco's "Opus one" hold music). The Moon Baby's falsetto takes up the hyper-femininity associated with the squeak of Lene's own singing. Unlike the strident, almost defiant, timbre of Lene's vocals, singing at this register takes on new vulnerability in The Moon Baby's trans-feminine interpretation.

The singing voice is an integral passage between dysphoria and affirmation for trans individuals who may feel alienated by their own vocal cords, even as they *finally* feel at home in their bodies.[6] In this performance, The Moon Baby's signature piercing timbre imbues this summer love song with new weight, particularly because many trans people find safety, desire, and respite on the dancefloor. Moreover, the pleas for diagnosis and a cure from our titular doctor take on important new valences when sung by a trans performer. Lene's lovesickness for her departed paramour turns inward in the cover, where navigating the medical industrial complex's pitfalls is the most expedient means for trans-self-recognition as a socially legible and lovable subject. But this cover does not leave the beleaguered queer listener to fend for themselves. The Moon Baby sings both the feminine and masculine vocals, though not to the same degree of intentional differentiation in Scotia's sultry treatment of "Barbie Girl," thereby furnishing a queer camp interpretation that upends the song's explicit heteronormative narrative as well as the slip into a medicalized

---

[6]Craig Jennex and Maria Murphy, "Covering Trans Media: Temporal and Narrative Potential in Messy Musical Archives," in *The Routledge Companion to Popular Music and Gender*, ed. Stan Hawkins (London: Routledge, 2017), 313–25.

trans discourse. There is parody here, but not ridicule. The Moon Baby's two-voiced-ness plays as "a borderline object that draws attention to the mutability of boundaries, be they boundaries between bodies or boundaries between the signifier and its origin."[7] J-cow flags the vocoded modifications by sliding the deeper register flat to evoke René's own campy performance. With the realization that The Moon Baby sings both parts, the cover's queer camp manifests as a love song to the multiple identities that exist in a non-linear temporal relationship to transness. Various iterations of the self stretch forward and backward across time in the dissolution of the gender binary that accompanies transition. In their cover, J-Cow and The Moon Baby employ camp's self-reflexive irony to eschew the song's maudlin longing for a faraway paramour in favor of a trans affirmation (that could never be *too* serious).

The video for "Doctor Jones" takes the song's evocation of distance to an exoticizing extreme. It was one of five from *Aquarium* directed by Pedersen and Stenbæk and is stamped with their hallmark Hollywood kitsch visual sensibility. It shifts from the hot pink and plastic of "Barbie Girl" to a generalized version of the colonial tropics florescent with artificial plants and polyester costumes that run from British safari to Tarzan-and-Jane. The video is a jumble of generalized colonial symbols taken from across the Global South: it opens in the Pacific; moonlight glints on the water's surface and cuts to Lene bedecked with a lei of artificial flowers entering the frame from behind a plastic palm tree as a model volcano erupts in the background. She adorns René with a matching garland before

---

[7] Jarman-Ivens, *Queer Voices*, 10.

they bid each other adieu. The shift from pre-chorus to verse signals a geographic swing from a timeless tropical isle to a generalized colonial Africa, with Lene incongruously dressed in an army camouflage cap-sleeved t-shirt. Our cast of characters is introduced over a title sequence montage of a double-propeller plane and its trajectory over the African continent before landing in the conveniently named city of "Aquaria." The title fades to Lene, Claus, and Søren, canoeing down a river, clearing their way through the jungle with machetes, and ferrying Lene's trunks across a swamp. These shots alternate with Lene and René longing for one another. Lene holds fast to a framed sepia-toned photo of her lover; René, cross-eyed with adoration, coochi-coos and kisses a voodoo doll surrogate. The intrepid explorers are ambushed by a group of scantily clad "natives," while a clueless René comfortably lounges in his tent. Lene, wearing impractically fashionable, animal print, knee-high platform boots, is strung across a pole and paraded into the village like a Looney Toons hostage. The appeals to Doctor Jones to "cure" her are translated into a panicked plea for her life and redirected toward the villagers wearing generalized "primitive" African masks (Figure 6). French subtitles speak for the chief: "Boys, we eat in eight hours . . . and you all are the dinner!" He produces two voodoo dolls and says, as streams of smoke miraculously spring from the ground, "But for the entrée, we'll have VOODOO!" As the hapless trio simmers in a cauldron, Doctor Jones finally heeds the calls for him to "wake up now," emerging from his tent to reveal he was in the village all along. After confirming that these are friends not food, Aqua "goes native" donning cheetah print tunics and plastic bone jewelry to play music for and dance with their new masked

Mais pour l'entrée, on prend du VOODOO!

Figure 6 *Still from Aqua's "Doctor Jones," screengrab by author.*

compatriots. The video ends with the picture-perfect scene of our reunited white protagonists who lean in for a kiss as an iris transition closes to black.

But from where might Pedersen and Stenbæk have drawn this juvenile colonial veneer when the song itself has no explicit connotation with "the tropics" beyond the evocations of summer warmth? One explanation is easy; at a superficial level, it is only a short step from the placeholder "Doctor Jones" to the Doctor Indiana Jones of Steven Spielberg and George Lucas's action-adventure trilogy.[8] While the interwar colonial styling and volcano certainly bring the exoticist kitsch of the adventuring American archaeologist to mind, none of the original Indiana Jones trilogy takes place in sub-Saharan Africa. At a more conceptual level, the geographic distance that characterized colonial communication may be associatively conveyed in the repeated set of triplets that comprise the song's bassline and are reminiscent of telegraphy's rhythmic dots and dashes, represented in the video as Lene and René tap their lyrics separated across the screen by a running ticker tape.

---

[8] Stenbæk, February 17, 2022.

Indiana Jones may have been a convenient subject for a spoof, but the video's cohesive narrative of romantic longing between geographically distanced white colonial subjects in East Africa during the early decades of the twentieth century tracks much more closely with a distinctly Danish reference, the colonial camp melodrama of the 1985 film *Out of Africa*. Based on the 1934 memoir of the same name by author Karen Blixen, played by Meryl Streep, the Danish Baroness establishes a coffee plantation in British Kenya where she meets her love interest Denys Finch Hatton, played by Robert Redford, an American big-game hunter who cannot be pinned down. Separation is at the heart of Blixen's account of Africa: at her wedding, which occurs mere hours after her arrival in Nairobi, her husband, the Swedish Baron Bror Blixen, cautions Karen to be kind to the minor colonial bourgeoisie she finds herself surrounded with because they are the entirety of Kenya's (white) society. In contrast to Karen's mostly stationary position, the men in her life come and go as they please and leave her to manage the coffee plantation alone. Karen also must depart from her farm run by Kikuyu laborers and return to Denmark to be treated for syphilis—the result of Bror's infidelity; a journey repeated as the film's denouement when, after the sudden destruction of the plantation in a fire and the death of her lover, Karen returns to her home country never to see Africa again.

Out of Africa's melodrama of European bourgeois love and longing at a spatial distance scaled to the colonized African continent offers an important parallel to the video for "Doctor Jones." Even the slight paternalism that produces the final plot twist in Aqua's video—René as an "expert" who can commune

I'm an *Exotic(izing)* Girl

with "the natives"—is reminiscent of both Denys, who works closely with Africans antagonistic to colonial contact, and Karen's establishment of a school to educate the Kikuyu laborers she refers to as "hers." The authenticity of the "good" colonizer is established through "genuine" communication with "the African" across cultural boundaries produced to reify hierarchies—we will soon see these scare quotes are also camp. Although Pedersen and Stenbæk hyperbolized this dynamic to the point of cartoon lunacy, it circumscribes a narrative of colonial racial dynamics on a dance track that barely had a narrative to begin with.

The video limits the interpretive valences of "Doctor Jones" by indulging a nostalgic colonial fantasy with a feigned naïveté that operates in the indeterminate space between camp and racist kitsch. Although the relationship between race and camp is oblique in Sontag's formulation and overwhelmingly unaddressed in queer reclamations, its racist potential is implicitly indicated throughout her "Notes." Sontag's most explicit evocation analogically illustrates her discussion of the "peculiar relation between Camp taste and homosexuality." Sontag says the homosexual desire to integrate into society through an aesthetic sense is parallel to Jewish liberal self-legitimization by way of moral sense. In both cases, the society referred to is implicitly a colonial one because, according to Sontag, "Camp taste is by its nature possible only in affluent societies, in societies or circles capable of experiencing the psychopathology of affluence." Camp is the purview of bourgeois subjects unable to fully claim cis-hetero whiteness, and, conjoined to its purported ethical neutrality and nostalgic impulse, allows affluent society's racist cultural objects to be folded into camp as "a mode of enjoyment, of appreciation—not judgement."[9] The proximity of camp to racist kitsch emerges when it is defined as an ameliorative relationship to affluent societies (i.e., the white colonial west) by particular constituencies who are socially marginalized yet economically privileged. Performance studies theorist Tavia Nyong'o applies racist kitsch to the form of stereotyped, vaudevillian representations of Black people as less than human things in the form of décor and "innocent" depictions of imperiled Black children like Topsy from *Uncle Tom's Cabin* or *The Story of Little Black Sambo*, a picture book from 1900. He claims that racist kitsch strives "to say something banal . . . to move unobtrusively among the objects of our everyday encounter" and that retroactive responses inspire a disgust that "apprehends the object as a kind of body that we are not" and "draws a boundary, not only against the object's complicit audiences, but also against the object itself."[10] If one is to take the small, but critical, step from kitsch to camp, the self-awareness required of the sensibility contorts the affect of disgust into the white tittering of irony. The video for "Doctor Jones" passes through colonial extraction in Africa, mediated by the temporal distance of a clichéd modernist safari aesthetics, by camping that violence as a zany and humorous misunderstanding between white and "native" cultures.[11]

---

9 Sontag, "Notes on Camp," 289–91.
10 Tavia Nyong'o, "Racial Kitsch and Black Performance," *The Yale Journal of Criticism* 15, no. 2 (Fall 2002): 371.
11 Sianne Ngai, *Our Aesthetic Categories: Zany, Cute, Interesting* (Cambridge: Harvard University Press, 2012), 181–232. For Ngai, the postmodern zany is also an important category for postmodern feminist critiques of gendered

"Doctor Jones"'s visual foray into nostalgic colonial fantasy inspired other Danish Bubblegum dance acts to try a similar formula. Toy-Box, the Aqua copycat band par excellence, amped up the racist camp of "Doctor Jones" in the guise of childlike naïveté with the single "Tarzan & Jane" from their album *Fantastic* released two years after *Aquarium*. Produced by Per Holm from Cut'n'Move, Toy-Box (vocalists Anlia Mirza and Amir El-Falaki) was a studio product of Spin Music!, and they wore their relationship to Aqua on their sleeve. One *Billboard* critic opens a review of the single by saying "You will swear this ultra-kitschy track marks the return of Aqua. . . . The formula here is identical: a husky, accented male vocal accompanied by a sweet girly-girl chorus." The critic goes on, "How you're likely to hear this depends wholly on your appetite for such cheeky zaniness."[12] Following the formula established by Aqua, Toy-Box's "Tarzan & Jane" heightens the naïveté of its colonial exoticism with a Bubblegum Dance sweetness. In this romance between colonial children in Equatorial Africa, Amir exaggerates Tarzan's "pidgin" English and punctuates the track with his signature "swinging-through-the-trees cry," as the reviewer described it. Anlia plays Jane and echoes Tarzan with her own call and coyly repeats "I am Jane and I love to ride an elephant." With juvenile lyrics, chimpanzee cackles, and a kooky video, Toy-Box eschewed Aqua's desire to straddle adult and tween listeners in favor of an appeal to the youngest market, as evidenced by the fact that the release of "Tarzan & Jane" was timed to coincide

capitalism precisely because of its ambiguous (but not indifferent) relationship to the performance of labor.

[12] Chuck Taylor, "Singles," *Billboard*, June 19, 1999, 18.

Figure 7 *Still from Toy-Box's "Tarzan & Jane," screengrab by author.*

with Disney's 1999 film *Tarzan* (Figure 7). Their producer did not shy away from this marketing strategy, saying, "We knew we were going to have problems with getting airplay on the radio and getting club play precisely because it is so young." Although the proposed "kindergarten tour" never came to fruition, "they actually held a press conference where no adults were allowed to come and ask questions, but instead only children."[13] Toy-Box's "Tarzan & Jane" therefore participates in a history of marketing naïve colonial aesthetics to children that was over a century long, and the reader of this racist kitsch, according to Tavia Nyong'o, "invents or produces race in an innocent text that is doing its best to get beyond, or outside, or before race."[14]

The juvenile and sentimental engagements with Africa in Danish Bubblegum dance seek to elide Denmark's own history of participation in the slave trade and colonialism. If the video for "Doctor Jones" is read against Toy-Box's exaggerated derivation, it reveals the use of camp's implicit capacity to

[13] Mads Kastrup, "Dansen om Dukkehuset," *Berlingske Tidende*, October 2, 1999, 2.
[14] Nyong'o "Racist Kitsch," 382.

enfold racist objects through the scare quotes of an irony that only goes halfway with its critique. Only by fully extricating the song from its video can any possibility of a queer camp, ethically motivated by a solidarity against the "affluent societies" it undermines, adhere to "Doctor Jones." While our first listen to J-Cow and The Moon Baby's cover hinged on the vocals' trans-camping of the song, its instrumentation may also go some way to disentangle the video's exoticizing camp from a queer musical one. Syncopated breakbeats, record scratches, and the deep kick drum rhythmically drive the cover. They are all quintessential elements of the liquid drum and bass (DnB) and Jungle subgenres that arose in London's Black British communities in the early 1990s.[15] Here, the video's visual stereotypes of a colonial African *jungle* are replaced by musical elements of *jungle* as a connection among Black Atlantic sonic cultures.[16] J-Cow's instrumentation pays homage to the centrality of Black British innovation in dance music to disarticulate the visual "tropics" without fully disavowing this element of the song's reception. This subtle queer inflection supplements The Moon Baby's interjection of a trans narrative element. These multiple significations are external to the original song itself, but nonetheless integral to its critical reception within the realm of queer camp. And these valences are not exclusive to "Doctor Jones," but proliferate on *Aquarium*, as we will see in the kinkier instance of "Lollipop (Candyman)" in the following chapter.

---

[15] Martin James, *State of Bass: The Origins of Jungle/Drum & Bass* (London: Velocity Press, 2020).
[16] For more information on Black Atlantic sonic cultures see, Paul Gilroy, *The Black Atlantic: Modernity and Double Consciousness* (New York: Verso, 1993).

5 I'm a *Hungry* Girl

Expectations were high when Aqua released "Lollipop (Candyman)" in the fall of 1997, the fifth single from *Aquarium*, and the second and final to chart in the United States. "Nothing like a sugar rush," wrote Dave Sholin, "and this is yet another double dose of ear candy from Denmark's leading confectioners." In just a phrase, he establishes a continuum with *Aquarium*'s impressive retinue of singles to playfully draw out a doubled slippage between musical and lyrical sweetness as a placeholder for the escapist pleasure that accompanies the satisfaction of the track.[1] Larry Flick, writing for *Billboard*, took a more hesitant stance, characterizing the single as derivative of "Barbie Girl" and "just as fun and goofy as its predecessor." This is "pop music at its most frivolous and disposable," he summarily concludes. Nevertheless, Flick cannot quite pin down the track despite a critical vocabulary that implies he was able to enjoy the single's zany freneticism and bracket its inanity with a push of the play-button. Interrogations, not assertions, conclude his review: "But who says every record needs to make a profound statement? Sometimes a fleeting record that inspires a grin or two is just as necessary as music of supreme relevance."[2] Flick's positive

---

[1] Dave Sholin, "Gavin Picks," *Gavin*, no. 2176 (October 10, 1997): 78.
[2] Larry Flick, "Singles," *Billboard Newspaper* 109, no. 43 (October 25, 1997): 79.

evaluation of the track because of its superficial frivolity implies an ironic sensibility that offers additional insight into Aqua's camp.

The distinct opinions of these two critics put a finer point on *Aquarium*'s capacity to exist in multiple pop spheres simultaneously because their saccharine frivolity and disposability imbue these thumping tracks with a chameleon's mutability. To be clear, these interpretations are not vastly different, much less opposed; both are brief reviews certain of Aqua's short shelf life. They take *Aquarium*'s singles to be emblematic of a juvenile worldview, enjoyable because of their outlandishness. On the one hand, Sholin relishes the deluge of an irresistible earworm confident that it will inevitably be replaced by another. On the other, Flick's assessment reads like a disingenuous smile that placates a precocious child. Yet the most important divergence between them relates to the song's commercial appeal when compared to *Aquarium*'s flagship effort. Flick's review opens with an inquiry: "Can Aqua do it again?" For Flick, the group's foremost challenge was to match their initial success with what he characterized as "a similar-sounding Euro-NRG ditty" that "does not have such an immediate media-friendly punch." Certainly, there is an unequivocal resemblance between Aqua's hits, but what does Flick mean when he finds the song lacks a "media-friendly punch"? Based on Sholin's remark that the track was "pulling enormous request action" relative to its predecessor, "Lollipop (Candyman)" clearly had commercial appeal.[3] This chapter argues the lack of immediacy that elicits the *Billboard*

---

[3] Sholin, "Gavin Picks," 78.

critic's pause is based on the coded queer fetishism and sci-fi aesthetics of "Lollipop (Candyman)" that sever it from the seeming singularity of US commodity culture.

"Lollipop (Candyman)" begins with an ethereal, spacy synthesized ground layered beneath a clavichord-esque melody—not dissimilar to the spinet synth that establishes the "old-timey" feel of "My Oh My"—that alternates on a fifth for a measure and a half. From this stable and elevated position, the second half of the four-measure melody line erupts with a run of sixteenth notes. Then enters Lene's voice, with a quartet of "oohs" that move up a third, then a sixth to resolve on the fifth interval, followed by René's unmistakably gruff introduction, "I am the candy man." Lene coos once more. "Coming from Bountyland," René replies as Lene's refrain repeats. "I am the Candyman," René reiterates and then pronounces in a declamatory staccato, "coming from Bountyland!" as the propulsive bass line blasts off like a rocket. Like most of the other hits from the album, "Lollipop (Candyman)" is an aural confection, sweet to the point of a diabetic coma, and follows the formula of alternating lines or verses between Lene and René. The result is a barely sensical narrative in which Lene and René (as the figure of the Candyman) present themselves as star-crossed lovers searching for a utopic Bountyland where they each become sweets for the other to voraciously devour. During a 1997 Canadian television interview, Søren confirms that the track is set in a special universe, "a love story explained through candy."[4]

---

[4]"Aqua Live in Montréal 1998—Barbie Girl," https://youtu.be/7Dze5jOddcQ (accessed June 21, 2023).

In this world's honeyed eroticism, however, the soda pop that grows on sugar trees spills into the kinky corporeality of this toothsome pair: Lene ecstatically fantasizes herself a piece of Bubble Yum to be macerated for hours and René reveals the Candyman's vorarephilic masochism wherein he pleads for Lene to ingest him entirely—"Bite me I'm yours if you're hungry please understand. This is the end of the sweet sugar Candyman."[5] Where the gender and dom-sub BDSM of the earlier "My Oh My" becomes clear only when song and video come together, "Lollipop (Candyman)" performs a fetishistic mutual self-annihilation on an inter-planetary scale.

If we push our reading a bit further, to embrace the overwrought ethos of Aqua themselves, there is a queerness embedded in this bubblegum single. With the articulated lust to ingest a sexual partner, "Lollipop (Candyman)" engages a less-trafficked fetish that emerged contemporary to *Aquarium*'s release in the 1990s. Although vorarephilia or "vore" fetishism certainly existed before the end of the twentieth century, contemporary instantiations of it in the form of written and visual fanfiction were uniquely facilitated by internet forums and the development of online communities. Aqua's "Lollipop (Candyman)" extends this fetish into the musical, with a throbbing bass that drives the lyrics and undergirds its ingestive demand. Vore fetishism nearly always entails a dominate-submissive dyad, like other BDSM cultures, in which the dominate partner (the predator) consumes the submissive (the prey) with a further distinction between violent mastication

[5] Amy D. Lykins and James M. Cantor, "Vorarephilia: A Case Study in Masochism and Erotic Consumption," *Archives of Sexual Behavior* 43, no. 6 (2014): 181–6.

(hard vore) and being swallowed whole (soft vore).[6] Satisfaction is often derived from a feeling of wholeness—the result of gluttonous satiation for the eater or complete envelopment for the eaten—that does not necessarily result in death but the "total destruction of being and personhood."[7] Vorarephelia is fundamentally tied to the Freudian "oral stage," the earliest erotic phase that ushers in a recognition of the contours of individual subjectivity among objects because it is structured by the distinction between consumption and deprivation.[8] While "normative" development prescribes a gradual shift to genital eroticism, vore porn offers a means to return to the fantasy pleasure of complete ingestion that has the power to blur the boundaries between individuals.

In "Lollipop (Candyman)'"s vore, subtext upends heteronormative "vanilla" sex where characters share a sweet tooth for a fatal *jouissance*. When both parties in this erotic exchange—perhaps the party is four if we count the implicit presence of Søren on keyboards and Claus on guitar—seek a ravishing obliteration through ingestion, the fetish breaks down. Yet, the extraterrestrial space of Bountyland unravels even the corporeal limits of vore sex and suggests a possibility as much in the music as the lyrics. As the song comes to a close, the chorus repeats itself to the point of fatuous redundancy, but with an important shift; the song's coherence begins to dissolve in the

[6]Richard Greenhill, "We Asked Predators and Prey About Their Vore Fetish," *Vice*, August 21, 2018, https://www.vice.com/en/article/vbj8dd/we-asked-predators-and-prey-about-their-vore-fetish.

[7]Lykins and Cantor, "Vorarephilia: A Case Study in Masochism and Erotic Consumption," 182, 184.

[8]Sigmund Freud, *Three Essays on the Theory of Sexuality*, trans. James Strachey (London: Penguin Books, 1977), 45–74.

final four lines, sung by Lene, as bits of phrases are chewed off, and words are swallowed until the song ends with the opening clavichord melody punctuated by a bass drum explosion.

It's all rather queer, no? A radically egalitarian exchange in which an ecstatic dissolution of subjectivity results from a digestive reciprocity that confounds the dynamics of straight sex floating on top of a club-ready beat. Might it be just this latent fetishism that unconsciously provoked Flick's concern that the song's syrupy metaphors lacked a "media-friendly punch"?

To a certain extent the *Billboard* critic's doubts about the commercial viability of "Lollipop (Candyman)" were substantiated in the United States, where the single only charted at 23 on the *Hot 100* and 24 on *Dance Club Songs*. Aqua hoped for more after the impact of "Barbie Girl," and in a recent interview attributes the modest reception of the single to a decision made by their American team at Universal. Søren remarks, "We didn't think that song was a hit." And that it "was a weird decision" to depart from other international strategies—where "My Oh My" and "Doctor Jones" preceded the release of "Lollipop (Candyman)." René and Lene agree, emphasizing the lack of control that they had over the decisions that impacted the global perception of the album. Lene remembers there being "so much politics at that point. . . . There were a lot of cooks in the kitchen, a lot of people that wanted to be a part of it, but the second single should have been left to us to decide."[9]

Outside of the United States, the single peaked at 38 on the *100 Hit Tracks* in Canada, topped out at 29 in France with

[9]Greene, "People Probably Want to Kill Us."

fourteen weeks on the charts, and spent thirteen weeks on the Swedish charts reaching number 10.[10] But no one seemed to love the track as much as the Australians, where the single stayed on the charts for eighteen weeks and was in the third position at its zenith.[11] Although Aqua was undoubtedly a hit in Australia (with five charting singles from *Aquarium*), the notable success of "Lollipop (Candyman)" may have been at least partially the result of the single's marketing strategy. The first tracks include the radio version, an extended play, and the anthemic "DJ Greek's Candy Remix," which inspires not a rush to the dancefloor but rather a resigned cringe, the result of poor beat matching that does a disservice to the original. Despite the lackluster remix, the second half of the CD-single ingeniously reminds listeners of the last single, "Doctor Jones," with a set of remixes that eclipse the disk's titular track. The single also included videos for both "Barbie Girl" and "Doctor Jones," and even "a cool Aqua Screensaver for use on your PC!!!!" as the cover exclaims. The Australian single was distinct in this marketing formula that promised, and delivered, a "media-friendly punch" sure to maintain the band's momentum Down Under.

But some clarity arrives outside of commercial sales, and in a deep cut made for the dancefloor. The queerness of erotic

---

[10]"100 Hit Tracks," *RPM*, January 26, 1998, https://www.bac-lac.gc.ca/eng/ discover/films-videos-sound-recordings/rpm/Pages/item.aspx?IdNumber =2131&; Les Charts, "lescharts.com," Last modified 2023, https://lescharts.com /showitem.asp?interpret=Aqua&titel=Lollipop+(Candyman)&cat=s.; Swedish Charts, "swedishcharts.com," Last modified 2023, https://swedishcharts.com/ showitem.asp?interpret=Aqua&titel=Lollipop+(Candyman)&cat=s.

[11]Australian Charts, "Australian-charts.com," Last modified 2023, https:// australiancharts.com/showitem.asp?interpret=Aqua&titel=Lollipop+ (Candyman)&cat=s.

ingestion and mutual self-annihilation manifests sonically beyond the song's coy double entendre in one remix for the 12-inch vinyl. The "Lick It" remix by Long Island–based house production duo Razor-n-Go stands out as exemplary insofar as it articulates the vorarephilic erotics of "Lollipop (Candyman)" by deprivileging the voice as a vehicle for conveying meaning. It favors a sensuous, abstracted, dance-driven soundscape that swallows the imagined club audience, transporting them to the rapacious "Bountyland" where bodies that come into contact on the dancefloor might be able to, however ephemerally, gain the ecstatic satisfaction of reciprocal "ingestion" and its queer erotics of dissolved personhood.

I was first enveloped by this remix in the belly of the beast. It was late on a mid-summer night at Les Souffleurs, one of the more queer-forward bars in Paris's Marais. The tiny basement dancefloor was packed, the perspiration and sporadic encounter with moist skin as intoxicating as the cocktail in my hand. And then the remix began. With a punctuated downbeat, a triplet, a high-hat to keep the tempo, and some bubbling bass, sounds that resemble Lene's voice began to emerge from the deep techno waters we unexpectedly found ourselves in. I wondered, as a deeper, pulsing synth kicked in, what word(s) were trying to escape this digitized and abstract feminine mouthpiece that became little more than an instrument in this remix. Perhaps we heard from the other side, from the inside, after having been consumed, luxuriating in the velvety belly of sound. (I speculate, but communicating across bodily boundaries is a common trope in vore porn.) The sharp staccato of the driving melody line dropped in right on cue, leaving little room to move beyond gyrating with the high-hat that keeps the twos and fours. A synth tympany held the ground while eyes scanned the room for dance partners.

Before I reminisce too long, the intestinal roiling suddenly stilled about seven minutes into this twelve-minute track, a wave that allowed for whatever breath one could find in the bar's humid depths. In the digestive abyss a triplet drumbeat punctuated this soundscape, followed by an eight-count of gravid silence, and another triplet on the four to maintain the interest of a queer mass of bodies undulating with and against one another. The tempo built and led us into a clearing where we could make out Lene singing "my love" on repeat before the music cuts again, and we were thrust into a palpitating bass. Yet the light of Bountyland's distant star still penetrated the surface, a shimmering synth to keep writhing club-goers tethered to the dancefloor. Here entered René's unmistakable voice repeatedly rasping "Candyman" amidst Lene's chopped-and-screwed enunciation of "my love." A driving melody forced its way into the remix as the words "candy man" and "my love" came in and out of focus. It grew sharper, keeping a pace impossible to sustain; the remix pushed us to the vorarephilic climax, an entrancing conduit to the satisfaction of imbibing the taste, touch, and smell of a stranger on a basement dancefloor illuminated by sidereal strobe lights. But as soon as we were sated, the party ends on a downbeat, and we were jolted back to earth from Bountyland. As the DJ reset the mood with a Thomas Bangalter house track, I took my cue to roll a cigarette (the ultimate post-coital cliché) and slip into the moonlit night.

My characterization of "Lolliop (Candyman)" as extraterrestrial, galactic, with an elevation, take-off, and a jet-fueled bass line against the song's confectionary lyrics is not pulled from thin air. Rather, it reinforces the integral connections between the visual and the sonic concretized by the accompanying music video. However, this sensory conjunction undermines the vore queerness implicit in the song itself and felt bodily with its club remixes. Although the sci-fi camp of the video moves against the lyrics (candy becomes a prop rather than the subject of the song), some inklings of queer potential remain in the visual manifestation of oral eroticism in "Lollipop (Candyman)" despite and because of the mediated screen of film between the spectator and the content of the song.

The video opens with Aqua's characteristic title sequence and thrusts the viewer into the vacuum of space amidst a computer-generated constellation of planets and stars. René's visage teleports front and center, a close-up shot lighting his face from various angles with colors that match the imagined solar system behind him. Cut to a gloriously cheap spaceship hurtling across the screen propelled by firecracker sparks and seemingly held aloft by some fishing line just out of view. As the song's melodic intro concludes, we are introduced to the band with René cast in the role of "Candyman" and a guest appearance from the goggle-eyed R2D2-esque robot named "C.A.N.D.Y." The shot cuts to the toy spaceship's interior where Lene acts as captain, singing directly to the viewer while Søren and Claus diligently twist an array of knobs and press a series of colorful buttons to keep the surfeit of gauges in equilibrium. René as Candyman suddenly appears on the screen and teleports aboard the vessel where he is greeted with exuberant waves, beckoning gestures, and a "modified"

Vulcan salute (here, with two in the pink one in the stink). C.A.N.D.Y. follows Candyman aboard and distributes lollipops in a gesture of goodwill. Lene looks out of the frame; she sensuously caresses her neck with the candy and dramatically extends her arm to underscore her command, "Oh my love, let us fly to bounty land." Meanwhile, Candyman pulls faces and jauntily wiggles his shoulders while licking with comical glee. This performative dichotomy, built upon the musical back-and-forth of the song, establishes yet another iteration of Aqua's playful engagement with pop music's gendered assumptions and the reversals camp affords.

As the first verse ends, the intrepid explorers disembark on what we take to be bounty land in identical Aqua-branded space suits and celebrate by dancing and playing a round of golf (Figure 8). Suddenly a gargantuan iguana appears behind a slime-green ridge, towering over the frightened band who flees from the foreground. This brief instance of digital compositing injects another layer of referential pastiche into the video, evoking Godzilla and playing with scale to dissolve the distinction between actor and model. The iguana signals

Figure 8 *Still from Aqua's "Lollipop (Candyman)," screengrab by author.*

a shift in the narrative as Aqua's revelry is interrupted by the planet's hostile inhabitants, little green men with glittering bulbous heads armed with fluorescent orange toy laser guns, who capture the band.

The scene shifts and Candyman's disembodied visage is reconnected to his captive body with wrists bolted to the wall behind him. As the camera zooms out, it reveals Lene strapped to an operating table, her body cloaked in rainbow light. Claus and Søren then come into view with their wrists fastened to the background wall, flanking René. The aliens poke and prod with mock aggression until the robot hero saves the day. Although armed with a rather threatening protuberance, C.A.N.D.Y. frees their companions with confectionary pacifism by firing a beam that transforms laser guns into lollipops. The denouement arrives suddenly, like the video for "Doctor Jones": Søren smiles and jigs with his captors although he is still shackled; Claus jovially embraces the alien jabbing him only seconds prior. Having delivered the joy of candy to the planet, Aqua is freed and the video ends with the planet's alien inhabitants joining the band in a dance party before they continue their exploration.

Despite the less-than-enthusiastic reflection on the video and single by the band and their team, the sci-fi visuals for "Lollipop (Candyman)" emerged from a broader technophilic cultural imaginary around the millennium and laid an influential foundation for other Eurodance engagements with the extraterrestrial in Denmark and across the continent. In some sense the hastily produced, low-budget video presaged stylistic engagements with the millenarian anxiety surrounding the "Y2K bug"—a projected limitation in computing calendar data after the year 2000 that threatened to throw worldwide infrastructures into chaos but resulted in fairly minor errors. Programmers had been theorizing the problem since the mid-1980s, but it flourished as a cultural phenomenon during the late 1990s as a container for anxieties around the potential failures of digitized neoliberal globalism, punctuated by the 1999 release of *The Matrix*. Music videos released around 2000 take up these techno-utopic visions for the new millennium with a range of aesthetic trends: shiny metallic fabrics and hairstyles that run the spectrum from sleek and slick hacker-chic to illuminated alien coifs (Whitney Houston's "It's Not Right But It's Okay" and Cher's "Believe"); cooled visual tones that cast everything in the clinical blue-white of a fluorescent tube; sets that evoke the metallic spaceship via airlocks (TLC's "No Scrubs" or Missy Elliott's "The Rain (Supa Dupa Fly)"), the conspicuous proliferation of surveilling screens and cameras (Céline Dion's "That's the Way it is" and Jennifer Lopez's "If You Had My Love"), or blur reality with the deep green of 8-bit computer screens (True Steppers & Dane Bowers featuring Victoria Beckham "Out of Your Mind").[12] These synthetic descriptions should all sound familiar after our reading of Aqua's video. More than merely locating a predecessor to these iterations of Y2K, Aqua furnished an alternative model that relished the low-budget, but not uncompelling, vision of an intergalactic human future. The distinct strain of camp sci-fi that emerged in the wake of "Lollipop (Candyman)" pinpoints another, underacknowledged facet of the group's impact on Eurodance during the period

[12] Geffen, *Glitter Up the Dark*, 200–18.

I'm a *Hungry Girl*

115

and draws out the uniqueness of the song's kinky relationship between music and visual.

Perhaps the most internationally recognizable example in this subgenre is Smile.dk's *japoniste* DDR-extravaganza, "Butterfly." Despite the ornamental domain name, Smile.dk was a Swedish girl group comprised of Veronica Almqvist and Nina Boquist. The video embraces the proliferation of CGI and green screen technology to build its digital and space-faring world, a departure from Aqua who opted for practical effect kitsch with "Lollipop (Candyman)"'s B-movie sensibility where set and scene readily bleed into one another. Set in a japanesque digital environment, Smile.dk is beamed from their red butterfly-hovercraft to the surface of a digital planet with a range of identical mountains in the background. The music video's narrative plays with the group's relationship to video game culture: the two singers traverse dimensions with the help of a butterfly-shaped "Samuradar" to discover the hidden unreality of this digital planet and complete their mission, that is to say they find boyfriends with whom they can resume exploration.

If we are to take a shared musical genre as a point of comparison, an underlying set of conceptual similarities emerges between Aqua and Smile.dk's space-themed videos. In their distinct modes, each employs blockbuster sci-fi tropes to engage the various hopes for and critiques of a technophilic future populated by aliens and machines. For example, Aqua's "Lollipop (Candyman)" shares with *Fifth Element* an incongruity between slick styling and slap-stick physicality to diffuse the anguish of a dystopian capitalist future. Smile.dk's dimension-jumping "Butterfly," with an eye always on Japan, more closely resembles a kitsch imitation of the cyberpunk allegorical investigation of human-machine interdependence gone awry in 1990s anime—think *Akira*, *Ghost in the Shell*, and *Neon Genesis Evangelion*. Cloaked in the up-tempo ebullience of Bubblegum Dance, both treatments of space present a happy ending and human-centered future at the precipice of a new millennium to combat increasing disillusionment with the 1990s neoliberal dream. Thinking beyond the limitations of the modern state via the conjunction of dance music and sci-fi was not unique to these groups For instance, Eiffel 65, the Italian trio with a computer-generated name, took a more somber approach with the almost entirely CGI-ed video of lumpy blue aliens for their minor-key earworm "Blue (Da Ba Dee)."

Unsurprisingly, it is Danish Bubblegum dance duo Hit'n'Hide's contribution to the trend of sci-fi visuals with "Space Invaders" that is most comparable to "Lollipop (Candyman)." Released shortly after their debut album *On A Ride* in the first half of 1998, the single and video for "Space Invaders" proved to be the group's biggest hit, spending seven weeks at number 1 in Denmark, making it to number 4 in Norway, and a respectable thirteen weeks in the top 20 on Sweden's charts.[13] The song's musical affinity with Aqua's Bubblegum dance is no coincidence because Hit'n'Hide moved in on *Aquarium*'s producers Karsten Delgado and Johnny Jam and their creative hand is present throughout. Jeanne C's vocals take Lene's high

---

[13] Danish Charts, "Danishcharts.com," Last updated 2015, https://web.archive .org/web/20151222144100/http://www.danishcharts.com/showitem.asp ?interpret=Hit+%27N%27+Hide&titel=Space+Invaders&cat=s.

register polished to a syrupy sweetness in the studio but lack the strident punch that cuts through the rich synthesized backing track. Morgan's deep and husky voice provides an excellent counter to Jeanne's soprano, but his delivery cannot quite match René's gravely earnestness mixed with a libertine humor. The song is staged as a dialogue between the vocalists: first, Jeanne makes a rather nonsensical pronouncement. Then, Morgan replies, often simply parroting Jeanne's line. A potential queerness marks the second verse: Jeanne begins, "You are an alien coming from the universe, trying to seduce every single man." While the gendered object of desire in this assertion just as easily refers to the masculine gender as well as the generalized form of the human, when sung to her deep-voiced companion it is peculiar that Morgan (playing the alien) ignores the suggestion of homoeroticism to transform it into annihilation: "We come from a galaxy where we don't like humanity; you cannot escape our master plan." Any allusion to queer inter-species sex is neutralized in Jeanne's final solo verse where she laments her love interest's departure "into hyperspace, back again to your alien girlfriend" and pleads for him to "stay for another day" before they fly away together.

Although Hit'n'Hide's song begs the question as to why we would presume aliens are dioecious, much less why they would only be interested in "straight" sex, the video transforms queer potential (however incidental) into violence and sublimates it to inter-species heterosexuality. Like Aqua's "Lollipop (Candyman)," Hit'n'Hide blended live action and CGI for the "Space Invaders" music video. The video largely centers on Jeanne's chatroom conversation with the aliens who threaten to invade earth. After pleading to join the extraterrestrial crew, we learn that the species can shapeshift into human form and, in fact, Jeanne herself is an alien. But the plot doubles back on itself, as Jeanne wakes up from her dream of alien transformation back in the real world.

Briefly setting aside the clichéd plot devices that fail to match Aqua's camp sensibility, Hit'n'Hide's single acts as a counterpoint to "Lollipop (Candyman)" because of its similarly oblique evocation of non-normative sex (by human standards) in a sci-fi future. Lyrically, "Space Invaders" hits the suggestion of queerness a bit more squarely on the nose with Morgan's seduction of "every single man." The video, however, inverts the narrative structure of the song to play up the allusion to a heterosexual love triangle. Heteronormative relations are visually reinforced with the early appearance of the unnamed woman with whom Jeanne C competes for Morgan's affection, implicitly the "alien girlfriend" from the third verse. Combined with the ubiquitous all-female crew who dances in the background, Morgan's persona shifts from a potentially queer alien visitor to an extraterrestrial lothario. The convoluted pantomime of the video's denouement augments this visual narrative and formally displaces the possibility of a queer alien future in a loosely dystopian mode. Ultimately the invasion that would consummate Jeanne's fantasy of alien copulation is denied and cannot be mourned. Compared to the latent kink of "Lollipop (Candyman)" that propels a peaceable resolution between human(oid) and alien, the conjunction of the sonic and visual in "Space Invaders" reifies binarized gender as a preordained function of any futurity: how bleak!

But does the queer consumptive kink of "Lollipop (Candyman)" make its way into Aqua's sci-fi video? The vorarephilia that bubbles beneath the surface of the song and its remixes seems entirely sublimated in the video; from a tale of erotic consummation to a hackneyed sci-fi drama wrapped up with a bow. Yet, our perplexing robot guest star provides a bridge between the sonic and the visual: C.A.N.D.Y. prestidigitates lollipops as a pacifying catalyst in each of the video's two major narrative moments—Candyman beaming aboard Aqua's spaceship and the crew's rescue from hostile aliens. Although these treats are certainly an easy means of clinging to even a loose connection to the lyrics, their narrative function draws the video back toward the song's linguistic and musical latent vorarephilic eroticism that filters the trope of space colonization through libidinal desire. The oral eroticism underlying "soft" vore extends beyond the relational pleasure of incorporating the desired object into the consuming subject. According to Karl Abraham and Melanie Klein, who each complicated Freud's foundational schema, the pleasure of oral consumption is accompanied by an aggressive, hostile *oral-sadistic stage*, more aligned with "hard" vore. Even the "soft" vore act of tenderly sucking (on a lollipop, for instance) "is accompanied by the destructive aim of sucking out, scooping out, emptying, exhausting."[14] Essentially, oral eroticism structures the subject's ambivalent engagement with the external world as a source of bounty and withholding,

---

[14]Paula Heimann and Susan Issacs, "Regression," in *Developments in Psychoanalysis*, ed. Paula Heimann, Susan Isaacs, Melanie Klein, and Joan Riviere (New York: Routledge, 2018), 186.

developed by the infant's relation to the mother's breast. Vore fantasy resolves the dilemma of oral eroticism by taking it to its queer extreme. The deprivations of the heteronormative external world that would starve the singular subject are rejected for the excessive fullness of mutual annihilation; the consumed sub and consuming dom constitute one another outside of the paternal phallus and maternal interior. The robot C.A.N.D.Y's confectionary interventions divert the video's plot away from a sci-fi recapitulation of interstellar conquest—a task "Doctor Jones" failed to accomplish. The inter-species camaraderie facilitated by the lollipop in Aqua's video retains the spark of a queerness from the ingestive envelopment that spells the end of "the sweet sugar candyman."

6 I'm a *Sentimental* Girl

At the height of their global fame, Aqua swept the 1998 Danish Grammys, winning seven awards including "Best Danish Group," "Best New Danish Band," "Best Danish Hit," "Best Danish Pop Album," "Best Music Video," "People's Choice Award," and the "P3 National Radio Listeners' award. In the span of only a year, Aqua's album had skyrocketed them to unfathomable heights. Riding the wave of their momentous success at home, Aqua resumed their tour Down Under. In March 1998, they played for 17,000 people in Sydney, Australia, where only a year before they performed for 86 people in Holbæck, Denmark. Their eighteen-month-long world tour ended in New Zealand where 25,000 people took to Auckland's main street to see the band.

Aqua may have concluded their tour, but their notoriety continued to grow. The ballad "Turn Back Time" was featured on the soundtrack for the British-American film *Sliding Doors*. The single, released just prior to the film's Sundance debut in January 1998, became Aqua's third number 1 hit in the UK and the sixth single from *Aquarium*. While this chapter focuses on "Turn Back Time," Aqua's most notable foray into something more somber, it was not the only ballad on *Aquarium*. "Good Morning Sunshine," the seventh and final single from *Aquarium*, was released in the UK in December 1998. These two tracks gave Aqua an opportunity to definitively dispel the presumption that they were just a "Barbie band" and showcase another facet of their sound. With adagio piano melodies, synth violin harmonies, saxophone bridges, and disco percussion, these ballads departed from *Aquarium*'s bass-heavy Bubblegum dance to offer poignant meditations on love, loss, and longing.

The video for "Turn Back Time" walks a challenging tightrope, balancing its ties to the motion picture, with cutscenes interspersed throughout, while also showcasing Lene's range and a more serious side of Aqua. Its subdued atmosphere might be surprising, given the fact that it was directed by Peter Stænbeck, who had been instrumental in the band's image from the start. Nevertheless, it successfully integrates Aqua into a narrative from the first scene that references the film's opening, a long shot along the length of a London tube platform, montaged with a cutscene of the station's sliding glass doors opening. The band strides into the station, all clad in black turtlenecks, button downs, and lapeled leather duster coats (Figure 9). Their somber sartorial aesthetic is

Figure 9 *Still from Aqua's "Turn Back Time," screengrab by author.*

complemented by the video's lighting. Stenbæk captured the affectively neutral functionality of underground public space by diffusing a cool blue-white light throughout punctuated with moments of intense overexposed whites that most often pull focus to close-up shots of Lene. In a music video tied to a film, Stenbæk adroitly asserts Aqua's authorship of the video with this set of slick clinical aesthetic choices that are all very *Matrix avant la lettre*.

The song stages a resonant scene of reflective melancholic regret and speculation about what could have been. Lene—who drops her signature ultra-high register for a breathy-yet-resolute soprano—opens the track with a plea for a scorned lover to "give her time" to symbolically turn back the clock and reflect on the season where she cheated on her partner. She poetically admits fault, singing "I will have a cross to wear, but the bolt reminds me I was there." She offers an aside asking for the strength "to face this test tonight" before a dramatic crescendo into the chorus. "If only I could turn back time," Lene's conditional lament is tempered by the song's major key and leaves open the possibility that she would not leave her scorned lover, but "stay for the night." The second verse takes a resolute and compassionate (or perhaps defensive) tone: Lene concedes that her lover should "claim [their] right" to what seems like an objective "truth." The subsequent couplet shifts the experience of pain from the transgressor to acknowledge the transgressed's perspective: "Though my pangs of conscience, will drill a hole in you." When Lene sings the final "stay" of the second chorus, a breakdown with staccato saxophone and juddering harmonic clangs serves as a bridge to a final repetition of the chorus. The song ends with the addition of a two-part male harmony sung by Søren that echoes Lene's forlorn "if only I could."

For at least one American reviewer, Aqua's endeavor to exhibit their versatility and range was unexpectedly successful. "Who didn't think the act that gave the world 'Barbie Girl' would be a one-hit wonder?" asks the reviewer for *Billboard*'s "Singles" column in January 1998, "Well here's what will likely be the third successful single from the Euro-dance act's massive album 'Aquarium.'" They assuredly claim it is "by far, the most credible pop offering by the set, with its shuffling faux-funk beat and sax lines." The critic's valuation of pop credibility here is intriguing because it is qualified with parameters external to the genre itself. We are pointed toward the sax line—its staccato jumps across an arpeggio more akin to smooth jazz—and a "faux-funk beat," which I take refers to the easy rhythm kept by a snare and high-hat. The review continues, "Everything about the track is surprisingly reserved—including the lead vocals, which are dramatically toned down from a kewpie-doll squeak to a quasi-soulful belt."[1] As we have seen, the assessment that Lene's vocals are a "squeak" followed the band throughout their rise to international stardom, was used to dismiss the band as a novelty, and ascribed the style with soullessness (as the obverse of a soulful belt). This negative connotation suggests a lack of pathos legible to a listener attuned to genres like rock, folk, and (of course) soul where a song's affective subtext is generated by the authentic "feeling" conveyed by a singer's voice. "A record to make top 40[;] sit up and take serious notice," the review prognosticates as its

---

[1] Larry Flick, "Aqua, Turn Back Time," *Billboard*, January 24, 1998, 57.

closing claim. Although the track topped charts globally, it never broke in the United States. I dwell on the disjuncture between this positive review from an American critic and the reality of the song's reception to reiterate a simple, but critical, facet of the band's significance in pop produced late in the last millennium: Aqua's *global* popularity was not solely determined by a rubric of popular taste predicated upon the perception that an artist's skill entailed an ability to cathartically connect with a listener. Rather, as this book continues to assert, the band's sudden ubiquity in 1997 and 1998 may in part be attributed to the effortless integration of musicianship and charisma into an expansively relatable exaggerated, bathetic naïveté, that is to say camp, in most of the senses laid out in the preceding chapters.

Even *Aquarium*'s most "credible" and "reserved" tracks still carry camp with them in the remix, despite (or is it because of?) the band's best efforts in 1998 to set in motion a shift away from the kitsch frivolity of Bubblegum toward pop music seen as having more heft. British production team Love to Infinity was brought on to give the song their signature treatment.[2] Love to Infinity remixed for the "who's who" of pop in the mid-1990s and early 2000s—Ace of Base, All Saints, Céline Dion, Cher, Madonna, and Michael Jackson, to name only a few. Known for their upbeat soulful House, Love to Infinity deftly distilled the core of global hits and effortlessly translated them for the dancefloor with dramatic whole-hand piano chord melodies, choral harmonies punched up to a gospel magnitude, and

---

[2] Anker, August 21, 2022. Anker noted that this was perhaps Aqua's most important remix in terms of critical acclaim.

infectious beats driven by synth claps and hi-hats. Their five remixes of "Turn Back Time" were no exception. Four of the five follow a similar format, with slight variations to accommodate adjacent genres: from the start, the "Master Mix" announces the presence of other hands on the production with synth snaps on the two and four, echoed slightly to multiply the hands in question. Perhaps picking up on the "faux-funk beat" that caught the Billboard reviewer's attention, the remix layers in a post-disco bass line with enough splat to keep the entirety of the five-minute-and-fifteen-second mix moving at an easy pace. Layered on top are some quintessential moog synth sounds characteristic of funk and imported into 1990s West Coast rap: including the portamento "whistle" of an oscillating sine-wave synth, and the shiny resonance of a chime keyboard that weaves through the middle frequencies. The "Thunderbird Mix" revs up the energy, opening with the sound of an alarm pulsing in the distance and a sharp synth stab. It abandons the song's balladic mood by chopping and repeating phrases, but maintaining a soaring breakdown resonant with the structure of the original track. Love to Infinity's slide between funk, R&B, and pop-inflected acid trance speaks to the chameleon-like malleability that augured Aqua's success even when shifted out of a Bubblegum mode. Yet, that nearly ineffable quality of camp remains and becomes perceptible in the harder "Thunderbird Mix." In this remix, Lene's "give me time" is repeated to build tension. However, as the line loops, it highlights the inkling of a quiver in Lene's voice as the pitch shifts up on "time." This quiver transforms the pining resignation of the original into a maudlin desperation disjoined from the heaviness of the remix and tints the drama of original lyrics with camp's "passionate failure" at seriousness that might be played with.[3]

Coming off their debut's run-away success over the course of 1997 and 1998, Aqua had big shoes to fill. When they retreated from the public eye to begin recording their sophomoric effort, these final two singles from *Aquarium* were meant to orient Aqua away from the saccharine frivolity and disposability of Bubblegum dance and toward the earnest, emotive sincerity of pop acts with staying power. Aqua shifted their approach when they began working on *Aquarius*. "When everyone else was going minimalistic," Søren recounts, "we thought, 'Why not go maximum?'"[4] The budget was bigger, working with a full orchestra and making one of the most expensive music videos ever.[5] The production changed; Delgado and Jam were replaced by a Universal Records team, including Stig Kreutzfeldt, a well-respected staple in the Danish rock-folk scene. And they sought to retain a sense of humor while also exploring the new directions that additional production resources might provide, emblematized by the album's lead single, "Cartoon Heroes." *Aquarius* was, however, by no measure a failed follow-up; it was the most purchased record in the Nordic countries when it was released in February 2000 and sold over eight million units worldwide.

Ultimately, Aqua's staying power on the global stage could not be sustained. The group performed a medley of hits during

---

[3] Sontag, 291.
[4] Rasted, October 10, 2022.
[5] Emma Garland, "How Aqua's 'Cartoon Heroes' Became One of the Most Expensive Videos Ever," *Vice*, July 17, 2017, https://www.vice.com/en/article/d38w7j/aqua-cartoon-heroes-one-of-most-expensive-music-videos-ever.

the 2001 Eurovision Song Context, with revised references to Barbie that elicited some controversy as their lawsuit with Mattel dragged toward a close. They split, abandoned a third album shortly after this appearance, and would not reunite until 2008. Aqua's fame was eclipsed after the turn of the millennium by a new cadre of European pop-dance crossovers indebted to their sound. They included the Danish duo S.O.A.P., who won an endorsement from Britney Spears with her b-side cover of their track "Deep In My Heart"; the Swedish A*Teens, who released an ABBA cover album before striking gold with their single "Upside Down"; and the international studio effort A Touch of Class (A.T.C.), famous for their non-lexical vocables in "Around the World (La La La La La)" and "My Heart Beats Like A Drum (Dam Dam Dam)." These acts represented a decisive shift in Bubblegum dance audiences, favoring an emergent tween market. Although Aqua was unable to maintain their explosive global success by shifting over to more "serious" and produced music, *Aquarium* lives on as perhaps the most influential pop-dance crossover album of its era. Around the twenty-fifth anniversary of its release in 2022, the album and its flagship single, "Barbie Girl," returned anew to the public sphere for listeners old and new. However, this book is not only interested in the waxing and waning position of Aqua in pop cultural consciousness. Rather, this history has attempted to elucidate Aqua's quiet endurance as an emblem of queer camp for over two decades. And it is here we will conclude.

Epilogue
I'm a *Happy* Girl

What if we closed this book with *Aquarium's* opening track, one of only four not released as a single? A synthesized jet-plane woosh and the thud of a kick-drum open the album before a chorus of voices (all of theme Lene's) cheerfully command the listener to "be happy." René twice suggestively adds, "Come on, let's go get it on," before clarifying, "Everybody let's go have some fun." Then enters a bouncy triplet bassline to give a bit of funk to the otherwise plodding four-four kick and perfunctory tambourine sixteenths. "Happy Boys and Girls" is a fluffy kickoff to *Aquarium* that is about just that, boys and girls having fun together at a party, making noise, throwing their hands in the air, and "break[ing] the ice" to flirt their way into the appropriately heterosexual couples alluded to by the dialogic structure of Lene and René's rapport.

"Happy Boys and Girls" ostensibly jeopardizes the queer camp subtexts I have argued might be excavated from *Aquarium*. When combined with the gender essentialism of "Be A Man," another non-single, the argument would seem further compromised. The track features a plucked guitar to tug at the heartstrings and Lene pleading with a lover who has left, "For once in your life, be a man. Just tell me the words, 'cause I know that you can." The two tracks' cringe-worthy heteronormativity lays bare the perils of queer pop cathexis. Melancholy inevitably accompanies the betrayal when your beloved objects cannot fulfill your desire for them to bring some levity and pleasure to a world that otherwise threatens, or at the very least ignores, your being in it.

However, might a queer sensibility be able to camp even these less savory deep cuts, shift them from their original context, and listen with gleeful masochism in the safe irony of quotation marks? The cover of "Happy Boys and Girls" by Chicago-based producer and DJ Ariel Zetina and vocalist Paula enthusiastically dives into the deep end in an attempt to queer even the straightest track on the album. Ariel foregrounds her own trans voice, or the trans and queer voices of others, in many of her projects. She has also worked as a trans voice coach and often draws attention to the voice as yet another site to play with the constrictions of gender by modifying it in post-production. She does not "improve" its "naturalness" within a gender binary but contorts and distorts the voice into a queer instrument all its own. Zetina provides the backing harmony for the cover and bends almost every pitch into a wiggling flow that is even more disorienting against her coyly blasé delivery. This foundation augments Paula's lead and their simultaneity collapses Lene and René's call-and-response. This composite dialogue unravels the ping-pong of gender in the original and where the grammatical construction of "happy boys and girls we'll be" becomes at once literal and metaphorical because queerness contains a multitude of genders that might cycle over time or be taken up and abandoned as they suit the wearer. Notably Zetina pairs down the instrumentation to draw further attention to the voice as a site of gender play with a violin melody line and a stronger four-four kick to propel the beat.

Zetina and Nacif's cover draws out a number of formal and symbolic trends that thread themselves across the covers analyzed over the course of the book. An ironic, yet also deeply sincere, embrace of a pop cultural object that would seem to demean, or at least ignore, queerness and transness is also felt in the covers of "Barbie Girl," where leaning into the bimbo becomes a way to affirm rather than undermine or critique queerness and trans-womanhood. A nonchalant, standoffish, or too-cool delivery of Aqua's lyrics is also evoked in the "Roses are Red" cover as KimKim and Proxy Server's vocals play up the pleasurable queer absurdity of a nursery rhyme on the dancefloor. And finally, the use of vocal modifications to play with the exaggerated heterosexuality of *Aquarium's* call-and-response lyrical structure resonates with the cover of "Doctor Jones" where the trans-feminine voice serves to dissolve into queer desire's multiplicity.

Then even one of *Aquarium's* least successful tracks slips back into the most generative realm of Sontag's camp: "[It's] not a woman, but a 'woman.' To perceive Camp in objects and persons is to understand Being-as-Playing-a-Role."[1] However, where Sontag reads this as a retreat from the political in favor of pleasurable artifice, to laugh with the performative reality of gender becomes a crucial site of exploration veiled behind irony for queer theorists and listeners.

This is precisely the aspect of Aqua's impact on contemporary pop culture that I have foregrounded throughout this book.

---

[1] Sontag, "Notes on Camp," 280.

The band's recent revival has secured their legacy, with a world tour, a four-part special on Danish radio, the inclusion of "Barbie Girl" as a sample on the soundtrack for Greta Gerwig's *Barbie*, and a remix of the track by world-famous DJ Tiësto. Nevertheless, the analyses at the core of the book's historical narrative furnish a new perspective on *Aquarium* because they rely on the sustained queer engagement with Aqua even when their popularity waned, *because* it waned, in the first two decades of the millennium. While the public may have pushed Aqua to the background, drag performers never forgot the appeal of donning a pink ensemble, bleach blond hairdo, and parodying the archetype of white womanhood. *Aquarium* has held a distinct place in the queer camp canon from its introduction to the North American market via gay clubs, to the bedrooms of queer tweens and teens figuring it out in the late 1990s, to its drop on the dancefloor of an underground queer party in Detroit, the birthplace of techno, in 2023.

Aqua's debut was a foundational node in the sonic landscape that bridged the optimism of the 1990s with the disillusionment that accompanied the turn of the millennium. To put this another way, the saccharine lack of criticality indelible to Bubblegum dance—with Denmark as the genre's most astute producer—served two separate functions on either side of the millennium. Its nonsensical superficiality fueled the exportation of 1990s rave culture into the consumerist mainstream as the perfect subcultural encapsulation of the era's positivity and excess that could speak to adults as well as tween consumers. With the increasing failures of late stage capitalism and neoliberal multiculturalism in the early

2000s—typified by the proliferation of xenophobia after 9/11 and the 2008 financial crisis—this same quality slid into a kind of Dadaist absurdity. These relations have been exacerbated for queers and might be typified by one trajectory: a 1990s activist demand for recognition during the AIDS crisis transformed into the sanitization of queerness later in the decade via the smokescreen of media acceptability (think *Will and Grace*, *Queer as Folk*, *The L Word*), which again shifted into the renewed push for political representation in the form of marriage equality (something contentious throughout the West), that produced visibility as yet another smokescreen of willing homonationalist assimilation (think *Queer Eye* and *Modern Family*).[2]

I make no claims to Bubblegum dance as an inherently subversive queer pop cultural form capable of intervening directly in post-millennial politics.[3] Yet, I do insist there is something powerfully queer about using the sweet, the frivolous, the camp, and the hyper (the feminine subtext to all these descriptors should come as no surprise) to cope with the ebbs and flows of hetero- and homonormative oppression and the interminably slow death of capitalism. And with my evocation of the "hyper," I have shown my hand.

The emergence of the hyperpop genre in the early 2010s emblematizes the legacy of Aqua and Bubblegum Eurodance

---

[2] On the connection between these various contemporary histories see Jabir K. Puar, *Terrorist Assemblages: Homonationalism in Queer Times* (Durham: Duke University Press, 2017).

[3] Geffen, *Glitter Up the Dark*, 219–21. Rather than equivocating, my position is akin to Geffen's optimistic pessimism around pop music's capacity for queer world-making.

with its proclivity for the repetition of catchy, saccharine lyrics; vocals auto-tuned to a slippery warble then pitched up to a squeak; and beats frenetic enough to exhaust even the most energized raver. Hyperpop is an aesthetic of excess and "joyful too-muchness."[4] It traffics in a nostalgia for the promise of the early internet's freedom from the vantage point of a post-millennial user attuned to online surveillance and capitalist encroachment. It performs a feminized cuteness explicitly informed by Japanese *kawaii* that is nevertheless tinged with something sinister by being too close to the desired object.[5] The relationship between these two characteristic excesses and *Aquarium*'s musical style, as a piece of Bubblegum dance more broadly, should be clear. What hyperpop adds to the mix is a distinctly queer sensibility that produces a self-aware camp criticality without compromising irony. As Szabo, the creator of the influential "hyperpop" Spotify playlist, puts it, "Hyperpop is a parody of pop. It almost pokes fun and pushes the bounds of that kind of quirky, traditional, radio popstar sound . . . [but] I think now you have a lot of creators who take it very seriously. This is not a parody, this is who they are, this is their sound."[6] Szabo describes the self-reflexivity of camp produced for an astute audience who is also in on the joke; a joke that Dorian Electra and Sega Bodega play up in their gratingly seductive trans-riff on Aqua with "Barbie Boy."

[4] Mark Richardson, "Hyperpop's Joyful Too-Muchness," *The Wall Street Journal*, December 29, 2020, https://www.wsj.com/articles/hyperpops-joyful-too -muchness-11609278593.
[5] Ngai, *Our Aesthetic Categories*, 53–109.
[6] Eli Enis, "This is Hyperpop: An Genre Tag for Genreless Music," *Vice*, October 27, 2020, https://www.vice.com/en/article/bvx85v/this-is-hyperpop-a-genre-tag -for-genre-less-music.

The camp and kitsch of hyperpop's stylistic markers are indebted to and entwined with the London-based label PC Music. Founded in 2013 by A. G. Cook, PC Music took an eccentric approach to electronic music out of step with both the mainstream and underground. They drew from a host of eclectic sources, "whether dance music subcultures that never entered the critical canon, like happy hardcore, or once-mainstream sounds that were otherwise written off as novelty, like Europop."[7] Combined with a flair for cheesy Y2K fashions that had not quite aged enough to attain the rarified status of vintage, the hyperreal femininity of PC Music stars like the tube-topped, hoop-earringed Hannah Diamond garnered direct comparisons with Aqua. "Like her previous singles," says Colin Joyce of *Spin* in 2015, "'Hi,' comes across like Aqua, if their liquid of choice was gasoline or Vaseline rather than pure old H2O."[8] The year before, Joyce penned another article comparing Sophie, the rising star of PC Music and now venerated trans-icon, to the Danish Bubblegum stars: "Today, they shared their demented first single, a fun house mirror version of something that Aqua (yes, the "Barbie Girl" dweebs) might have put out."[9] Though dismissive, Joyce hears Sophie's musically erudite camp riffs on what was seen as the

[7] Selim Bulut, "The History of PC Music, the Most Exhilarating Record Label of the 2010s," *Dazed Digital*, December 20, 2019, https://www.dazeddigital.com /music/article/47273/1/pc-music-a-g-cook-history-end-of-decade-2010s -retrospective.

[8] Colin Joyce, "Hannah Diamond Says 'Hi' with a Confetti-Filled Video," *Spin*, November 2, 2015, https://www.spin.com/2015/11/hannah-diamond-hi -video-watch/.

[9] Colin Joyce, "Like Aqua's Barbie Girl through a Funhouse Mirror, Meet SOPHIE," *Spin*, August 26, 2014, https://www.spin.com/2014/08/qt-hey-sophie-pc -music-stream-primer-label/.

Epilogue

detritus of late 1990s pop culture in the twilight of rock's "indie" revival in the 2000s. Sophie takes *Aquarium's* signature moves (traced throughout this book) and camps them into a queer avant-garde. Squelchy yet scintillating, dissonant yet catchy, frivolous yet profound, and all condensed into bite-size pop confections, reflecting on Sophie's oeuvre in the wake of her untimely death in 2021 speaks to Aqua's ongoing influence in queer electronic music, however sublimated. Her production epitomizes the post-millennial queer, and distinctly trans, capacity to camp cultural objects already deemed cringe beyond reclamation.

The covers integrated throughout the book concretize and expand upon Aqua's recursive influence on queer electronic music. In addition to the too-muchness of hyperpop, Aqua's Bubblegum dance has resonances with genres as far-reaching as trance, industrial, new wave, and liquid drum and bass. Each iteration of this queer approach to Aqua, including the methodology of this book itself, stands together insofar camp's ironic distance serves as a mechanism to articulate closeness legible outside the normative structures that would oppress; a doubled irony given the fact that the objects retooled to obliquely state that intimacy fall back into heteronormativity. So, it seems that among the multiple lives Aqua's *Aquarium* has had and will have, at least one is the making of happy "boys" and "girls"... and theys, and any other gender one might inhabit in this fantastic life in plastic.

Works Cited

Interviews

Anker, Niclas. Interview with the Author. February 4, 2022.
Anker, Niclas. Interview with the Author. August 21, 2022.
Anker, Niclas. Interview with the Author. August 31, 2022.
Delgado, Karsten. Interview with the Author. February 11, 2022.
Dif, Rene, Lene Nystrøm and Søren Rasted. "Hvem er Aqua? 1:4."
    Interview by Søren Bygbjerg. *Hvem er?* DR Lyd, September 30,
    2022. Audio, 52:00. https://www.dr.dk/lyd/p3/hvem-er/hvem
    -er-aqua-1-4.
Dif, Rene, Lene Nystrøm and Søren Rasted. "Hvem er Aqua? 2:4."
    Interview by Søren Bygbjerg. *Hvem er?* DR Lyd, September 30,
    2022. Audio, 51:00. https://www.dr.dk/lyd/p3/hvem-er/hvem
    -er-aqua-2-4.
Dif, Rene, Lene Nystrøm and Søren Rasted. "Hvem er Aqua? 3:4."
    Interview by Søren Bygbjerg. *Hvem er?* DR Lyd, September 30,
    2022. Audio, 60:01. https://www.dr.dk/lyd/p3/hvem-er/hvem
    -er-aqua-3-4.
Dif, Rene, Claus Norreen, Lene Nystrøm and Søren Rasted.
    Interview by Launch. *Launch.* 1997. Video. https://www
    .youtube.com/watch?v=O1DqXPU8Hcg.
Nakamoto, Tatsu. Interview with the Author. February 15, 2022.
Nystrøm, Lene. Interview with the Author. October 13, 2022.
Paludan, Jens-Otto. Interview with the Author. February 18, 2022.
Rasted, Søren. Interview with the Author. October 10, 2022.
Stenbæk, Peter. Interview with the Author. February 17, 2022.

Primary Literature

"100 Hit Tracks." *RPM* 66, no. 18 (January 26, 1998). https://www
.bac-lac.gc.ca/eng/discover/films-videos-soundrecordings/
rpm/Pages/item.aspx?IdNumber=2131&.

Abbott, Simon et al. "Single of the Week." *Music Week*, October 4,
1997.

"Airborne." *Music & Media* 15, nos. 1–3 (January 17, 1998).

"Aqua Live in Montréal 1998—Barbie Girl." https://www.youtube
.com/watch?v=7Dze5jOddcQ (accessed June 21, 2023).

Australian Charts. "Australian-charts.com." Last modified 2023.
https://australiancharts.com/showitem.asp?interpret=Aqua
&titel=Lollipop+(Candyman)&cat=s.

Browne, David. "Album Review: Aquarium." *Entertainment Weekly*,
October 17, 1997.

Danish Charts. "Danishcharts.com." Last updated 2015. https://
web.archive.org/web/20151222144100/http:/www
.danishcharts.com/showitem.asp?interpret=Hit+%27N%27
+Hide&titel=Space+Invaders&cat=s.

"Eka's Portal." *Aryion*. 2012. https://aryion.com/#show-forum-tree
(accessed June 23, 2023).

Ferro, Charles. "Danish Delight in Eastern Promise." *Music and
Media* 14, no. 18 (May 3, 1997): 16.

Ferro, Charles. "Global Music Pulse, Denmark." *Billboard*, March 29,
1997.

Flick, Larry. "Aqua, Turn Back Time." *Billboard*, January 24, 1998.

Flick, Larry. "New and Noteworthy." *Billboard*, August 16, 1997.

Flick, Larry. "Singles." *Billboard Newspaper*, October 25, 1997.

Hyman, James. "Hot Vinyl: Tune of the Week." *Music Week*,
September 13, 1997.

Kastrup, Mads. "Dansen om Dukkehuset." *Berlingske Tidende*,
October 2, 1999.

Les Charts. "lescharts.com." Last modified 2023. https://
lescharts.com/showitem.asp?interpret=Aqua&titel
=Lollipop+(Candyman)&cat=s.

Mattel, Inc. v. MCA Records, Inc., No. CV 97-6791-WMIB, 1998 U.S.
Dist. LEXIS 7310, at *6 (February 19, 1998).

Mattel, Inc. v. MCA Records, Inc., 28 F. Supp. 2d 1120 at 1125 (July
30, 1998).

Mattel, Inc. v. MCA Records, Inc. 296 F.3D (9th Cir.) "Opinion," VI
(July 24, 2002).

Nielsen, Reinholdt. "Bare Barbie kunne synge." *Berlingske Tidende*,
April 6, 1997.

Poulsen, Morton V. "Vand i hovedet." *Ekstra Bladet*, April 17, 1997.

"Roland Super JV1080: Expandable Synthesizer Module." *Sound
on Sound*. December 1994. https://www.soundonsound.com/
reviews/roland-super-jv1080.

"RPM Dance." *RPM Weekly*, March 23, 1998.

Sandiford-Waller, Theda. "Hot 100 Singles Spotlight." *Billboard*,
August 16, 1997.

Sandiford-Waller, Theda. "Hot 100 Singles Spotlight." *Billboard*,
August 19, 1997.

Sandiford-Waller, Theda. "Hot 100 Singles Spotlight." *Billboard*,
September 27, 1997.

Sholin, Dave. "Gavin Picks." *Gavin*, no. 2176, October 10, 1997.

Skotte, Kim. "Pop der holder vand." *Politiken*, March 25, 1997.

Smith, Gary. "Danish 'tackno' Brings Home the Bacon." *Music and
Media* 15, no. 15 (April 11, 1998): 7.

Swedish Charts. "swedishcharts.com." Last modified 2023. https://
swedishcharts.com/showitem.asp?interpret=Aqua&titel
=Lollipop+(Candyman)&cat=s.

Taylor, Chuck, ed. "Singles." *Billboard*, June 19, 1999.

The Aqua Diary: The Official Aquarium Home Video. Directed by
Peder Pedersen. Australia: Universal Music Group, 1998. VHS.

Secondary Literature

Alaimo, Stacy. *Bodily Nature: Science, Environment, and the Material Self*. Bloomington: University of Indiana Press, 2010.

Amin, Kadji. "Trans* Plasticity and the Ontology of Race and Species." *Social Text* 143 (2020): 49–71.

Auslander, Philip. *Performing Glam Rock: Gender and Theatricality in Popular Music*. Ann Arbor: University of Michigan Press, 2006.

Baker, Paul. *Camp!: The Story of the Attitude that Conquered the World*. London: Footnote Press, 2023.

Bick, Emily. "A Two Dimensional Matrix: Carl Stone speaks to Emily Bick." *The Wire*, March 2019. https://www.thewire.co.uk/in-writing/interviews/carl-stone-interview-by-emily-bick.

Bickford, Tyler. *Tween Pop*. Durham: Duke University Press, 2020.

Brostoff, Marissa. "Notes on Caitlyn, or Genre Trouble: On the Continued Usefulness of Camp as Queer Method." *differences: A Journal of Feminist Cultural Studies* 28, no. 3 (2017): 1–18.

Bruster, Bill and Frank Broughton. *Last Night a DJ Saved My Life: The History of the Disc Jockey*. New York: Grove Press, 2006.

Bulut, Selim. "The History of PC Music, the Most Exhilarating Record Label of the 2010s." *Dazed Digital*, December 20, 2019. https://www.dazeddigital.com/music/article/47273/1/pc-music-a-g-cook-history-end-of-decade-2010s-retrospective.

Burns, Todd L. "Charting Carl Stone's Musical Evolution: Sampling the Sacred and Profane." *Red Bull Music Academy*, December 5, 2016. https://daily.redbullmusicacademy.com/2016/12/carl-stone-interview/.

Butler, Judith. *Gender Trouble: Feminism and the Subversion of Identity*. New York: Routledge, 1990.

Cleto, Fabio. *Camp: Queer Aesthetics and the Performing Subject, A Reader*. Ann Arbor: University of Michigan Press, 1999.

Cooper, Kim and David Smay, eds. *Bubblegum Music, is the Naked Truth*. Los Angeles: Feral House, 2001.

Cunningham, Sid. "'Something to disclose'—Notes on *Disclosure and the Possibility of Trans Camp*." *Jump Cut: A Review of Contemporary Media*, no. 60 (Spring 2021). https://www.ejumpcut.org/archive/jc60.2021/Cunningham-Disclosure/index.html.

Dyer, Richard. *Heavenly Bodies: Film Stars and Society*. New York: St. Martin's Press, 1986.

Enis, Eli. "This is Hyperpop: A Genre Tag for Genreless Music." *Vice*, October 27, 2020. https://www.vice.com/en/article/bvx85v/this-is-hyperpop-a-genre-tag-for-genre-less-music.

Feldman, Jamie. "The Incredible True Story of How a College Student Launched Roxette To Fame In The U.S." *Huffington Post*, December 12, 2019. https://www.huffpost.com/entry/dean-cushman-roxette_n_5df00aa5e4b0a59848d1e559.

Freud, Sigmund. *Three Essays on the Theory of Sexuality*, trans. James Strachey. London: Penguin Books, 1977.

Freud, Sigmund. *Totem and Taboo*. London: Routledge Classics, 2001.

Freeman, Elizabeth. *Time Binds: Queer Temporalities, Queer Histories*. Durham: Duke University Press, 2010.

Frith, Simon. *Performing Rites: On the Value of Popular Music*. Cambridge: Harvard University Press, 1998.

Garland, Emma. "How Aqua's 'Cartoon Heroes' Became One of the Most Expensive Videos Ever." *Vice*, July 17, 2017. https://www.vice.com/en/article/d38w7j/aqua-cartoon-heroes-one-of-most-expensive-music-videos-ever.

Geffen, Sasha. *Glitter Up the Dark: How Pop Music Broke the Binary*. Austin: University of Texas Press, 2020.

Gilroy, Paul. *The Black Atlantic: Modernity and Double Consciousness*. New York: Verso, 1993.

Greene, Andy. "'People Probably Want to Kill Us': The Oral History of Aqua's 'Barbie Girl.'" *Rolling Stone*, April 1, 2022. https://www.rollingstone.com/music/music-features/aqua-barbie-girl-oral-history-1319069/.

Greenhill, Richard. "We Asked Predators and Prey About Their Vore Fetish." *Vice*, August 21, 2018. https://www.vice.com/en/article/vbj8dd/we-asked-predators-and-prey-about-their-vore-fetish.

Haraway, Donna. *Simians, Cyborgs, and Women: The Reinvention of Nature*. New York: Routledge, 1991.

Hawkins, Stan. *Queerness in Pop Music: Aesthetics, Gender Norms, and Temporality*. New York: Routledge, 2016.

Hawkins, Stan, ed. *The Routledge Companion to Popular Music and Gender*. London: Routledge, 2017.

Heimann, Paula, Susan Isaacs, Melanie Klein, and Joan Riviere, eds. *Developments in Psychoanalysis*. New York: Routledge, 2018.

Horn, Katrin. *Women, Camp, and Popular Culture: Serious Excess*. London: Palgrave MacMillan, 2017.

Hutcheon, Linda. *The Theory of Parody: The Teachings of Twentieth-Century Art Forms*. New York: Methuen, 1985.

Isherwood, Christopher. *The World in the Evening*. New York: Noonday Press, 1954.

James, Martin. *State of Bass: The Origins of Jungle/Drum & Bass*. London: London Velocity Press, 2020.

Jarman-Ivens, Freya. "Notes on Musical Camp." In *The Ashgate Research Companion to Popular Music*, edited by Derek B. Scott. Burlington, VT: Ashgate Publishing, 2009.

Jarman-Ivens, Freya. *Queer Voices: Technologies, Vocalities, and the Musical Flaw*. New York: Palgrave MacMillan, 2011.

Jarman-Ivens, Freya and Santiago Fouz-Hernandez, eds. *Madonna's Drowned Worlds: New Approaches to her Cultural Transformations, 1983–2003*. Burlington: Ashgate, 2004.

Joyce, Colin. "Hannah Diamond Says 'Hi' with a Confetti-Filled Video." *Spin*, November 2, 2015. https://www.spin.com/2015/11/hannah-diamond-hi-video-watch/.

Joyce, Colin. "Like Aqua's 'Barbie Girl' Through a Funhouse Mirror, Meet Sophie." *Spin*, August 26, 2014. https://www.spin.com/2014/08/qt-hey-sophie-pc-music-stream-primer-label/.

Legal Information Institute. "Parody." Cornell University Law School. https://www.law.cornell.edu/wex/parody (accessed June 21, 2023).

Lykins, Amy D. and James M. Cantor. "Vorarephilia: A Case Study in Masochism and Erotic Consumption." *Archives of Sexual Behavior* 43, no. 6 (2014): 181–6.

Meyer, Moe. *The Poetics and Politics of Camp*. New York: Routledge, 1994.

Moore, Christopher and Philip Purvis, eds. *Music & Camp*. Middletown, CT: Wesleyan University Press, 2018.

Muñoz, José Esteban. *Disidentifications: Queers of Color and the Performance of Politics*. Minneapolis: University of Minnesota Press, 1999.

Navas, Eduardo. *Remix Theory: The Aesthetics of Sampling*. New York: Springer, 2012.

Nawrot, Elizabeth. "The Perception of Emotional Expression in Music: Evidence from Infants, Children and Adults." *Psychology of Music* 31, no. 1 (2003): 75–92.

Ngai, Sianne. *Our Aesthetic Categories: Zany, Cute, Interesting*. Cambridge: Harvard University Press, 2015.

Nyong'o, Tavia. "Racial Kitsch and Black Performance." *The Yale Journal of Criticism* 15, no. 2 (Fall 2002): 371–91.

Oteri, Frank J. "Carl Stone: Intellectual Property, Artistic License and Free Access to Information in the Age of Sample-Based Music and the Internet." *American Music Center*, October 17, 2000.

"Pornostjerner i poolen." *Vild Med Dance*. DR. Episode 3. Audio, 29:00. June 29, 2021. https://www.dr.dk/drtv/episode/vild -med-dance-_-lyden-af-90erne_-pornostjerner-i-poolen _258835.

Provenzano, Catherine. "Making Voices: The Gendering of Pitch Correction and the Auto-Tune Effect in Contemporary Pop Music." *Journal of Popular Music Studies* 31, no. 2 (2019): 63–84.

Puar, Jasbir K. "I'd Rather Be A Cyborg Than a Goddess: Becoming Intersectional in Assemblage Theory." *Philosophia* 2, no. 1 (2012): 49–66.

Puar, Jabir K. *Terrorist Assemblages: Homonationalism in Queer Times*. Durham: Duke University Press, 2017.

Reynolds, Simon. *Energy Flash: A Journey Through Rave Music and Culture*. Berkeley: Stoft Skull Press, 2012.

Richardson, Mark. "Hyperpop's Joyful Too-Muchness." *The Wall Street Journal*, December 29, 2020. https://www.wsj.com/ articles/hyperpops-joyful-too-muchness-11609278593.

Robertson, Pamela. *Guilty Pleasures: Feminist Camp from Mae West to Madonna*. Durham: Duke University Press, 1996.

Ross, Andrew. *No Respect: Intellectuals and Popular Culture*. New York: Taylor and Francis, 1989.

Siu, Tik-Sze Carrey and Him Cheung. "Infants' Sensitivity to Emotion in Music and Emotion-Action Understanding." *PLoS One* 12, no. 2 (2017). https://doi.org/10.1371/journal.pone .0171023.

Sontag, Susan. *Against Interpretation and Other Essays*. New York: Farrar, Straus, and Giroux, 1966.

Sørenssen, Ingvild Kvale. "Disney's *High School Musical* and the Construction of the Tween Audience." *Global Studies of Childhood* 8, no. 3 (September 2018): 213–24.

Sørenssen, Ingvild Kvale. "Domesticating the Disney Tween Machine: Norwegian Tweens Enacting Age and Everyday Life."

PhD diss., Norwegian University of Science and Technology, 2014.

Steblin, Rita. *A History of Key Characteristics in the Eighteenth and Early-Nineteenth Centuries*. Ann Arbor: UMI Research Press, 1983.

Stryker, Susan. *Transgender History: The Roots of Today's Revolution*. 2nd edn. Berkeley: Seal Press, 2009.

Swift, Jacqui. *Aqua: The Official Book*. London: Virgin Books, 1998.

Taylor, Jodi. *Playing it Queer: Popular Music, Identity, and Queer World-Making*. New York: Peter Lang, 2012.

Vaccaro, Jeanne. "Feeling Fractals: Wooly Ecologies of Transgender Matter." *GLQ: A Journal of Lesbian and Gay Studies* 21, nos. 2–3 (2015): 273–93.

Warner, Michael. *Publics and Counterpublics*. New York: Zone Books, 2002.

White, William. "'Camp' as Adjective: 1909–1966." *American Speech* 41, no. 1 (1966): 70–2.

Wilson, Kat. "The Heartbreak Key: D Minor Plays on Our Rawest Emotion — But in Contemporary Music, Even the Most Somber of Artists Tend to Avoid It." *Rolling Stone*, August 18, 2021. https://www.rollingstone.com/pro/features/music-d -minor-saddest-key-1210591/.

Index